Shakespeare's
Greenwood

Crowdy & Loud

Shakespeare's Greenwood
The Customs of the Country

The Language; The Superstitions; The Customs; The Folk-Lore; The Birds & Trees; The Parson; The Poets; The Novelist

By George Morley

Author of "Leafy Warwickshire," "In Rustic Livery" "In Russet Mantle Clad," "Sweet Audrey" &c. &c.

HASKELL HOUSE PUBLISHERS LTD.
Publishers of Scarce Scholarly Books
NEW YORK. N. Y. 10012
1972

First Published 1900

HASKELL HOUSE PUBLISHERS LTD.
Publishers of Scarce Scholarly Books
280 LAFAYETTE STREET
NEW YORK, N. Y. 10012

Library of Congress Catalog Card Number: 70-185021

Standard Book Number 8383-1381-7

Printed in the United States of America

To
Marie Corelli
Sojourner at Ye Hall's Croft, Stratford-on-Avon
In token of
Her love for Shakespeare's Greenwood
My warmest thanks and
This Book

GEORGE MORLEY

Sunnyside, Leamington
1900

Preface

A portion of this work originally appeared in an abbreviated form in the pages of Knowledge, Country Life, *and* The Art Journal. *Amplified and improved, I now present this book to the public in the belief that it depicts the chief and most interesting phases of old-time feeling and custom still surviving in modern life and to be still observed among the dwellers in the picturesque villages of Shakespeare's Greenwood; in fact, is the only book of its kind yet issued.*

GEORGE MORLEY

Sunnyside, Leamington
1900

Illustrations

By Caroline Watts

Shakespeare's Bust	*Frontispiece*
Shakespeare's Cottage	*Page* 1
Ann Hathaway's Cottage	61
Shakespeare's Birth Room	101
The Deer-stealing Room at Charlecote	151
A Warwickshire Landscape	185
A Woodland Scene	217
Arbury Hall ("Cheverel Manor")	259

Contents

The Language — Page 1

The Forest of Arden	3
"Hungry Harbury"	9
The Harbury Carrier	10
The Blue Biggen	11
The Reckling and Dilling	13
The Nesh Child	15
The Frem Child	15
The Wench	17
The Faggot	19
The Slummock	21
Hedgehog and Urchin	22
Terms of Punishment	23
Shog and Shogged	24
"Lobb's Courtship"	25
A Shive	26
The T sound for D	28

Contents

	Page
Call ("No Call to")	29
To Fend	31
"Shakespeare Hall" (where Shakespeare wrote his Sonnets)	32
Flower Names	33
"Naked Ladies"	35
A Blench	36
On for of	36
The Butty	38
To Cumber	38
Moither, Mummock, or Moil	39
The Batlet (of Jane Smile)	42
The Dag	43
The Anointed Scaramouch	44
The Cade Lamb	45
"This Fore-Wearied Flesh"	46
O for W ("Wuts" for Oats)	46
Rimming	48
Unked	48
To Favour or Judge	49
"The Ten Commandments"	51
The Deaf-Nut	51
Tooting	53
Brevetting	53
Othergates	54
A Colly Day	54

Contents

Mortal in Love or Folly (the Poetry of the Language) *Page*	55
The Close Alliance of the Dialect to the Bible and Shakespeare	57

The Superstitions 59

The Vale of the Red Horse	62
The Fateful Magpie	63
The Rollright Stones	65
The Last Warwickshire Witch	66
The Famous Witch-Sticking at Long Compton and Tysoe	69
The Ilmington Hills	71
The Devil in Ilmington	72
The Poisoning of Sir Thomas Overbury (a Native)	72
The Night Coach and Night Hounds	73
One-Handed Boughton	75
His Ghost caught in a Phial and "laid" in a Marl Pit	75
Seeing the Phantom Coach-and-Six	77
Mr. Snell's Opinion	79
Squire Newsham's Ghost and Night Coach	80
The Superstitions of Guy's Cliffe	83

The Ghost of Piers Gaveston *Page*	84
The Ghostly Procession to Blacklow Hill	85
The White Woman of Chesford Bridge	87
The Dial House Murder	88
The Murder at Littleham Bridge	89
The Hole that cannot be Filled	89
Clopton House	90
The Tragic Death of Charlotte Clopton (the Juliet of Shakespeare)	91
The Clopton Vault in Stratford-on-Avon Church	92
The Drowning of Margaret Clopton (the Ophelia of Shakespeare)	93
The Murder of a Monk in Clopton Oratory	94
The Spirit of the Wych Elm	95

The Customs — 99

Street Football at "Milby" (Nuneaton) on Shrove Tuesday	102
The Mothering	103
The Mothering Dishes (Stuffed Chine of Pork and Fig Pudding)	105
The Easter Lifting	106

Contents xiii

The Lifting and Kissing of Dr. Samuel Parr, LL.D. *Page*	107
The Maying	107
The Maying Songs	108
The Shakespeare Maypole at Welford	110
The Sea-Gulls and Schoolboys of Oakfield	111
The Beating of the Bounds	112
Drum-Beating at Arbury Hall (The "Cheverel Manor" of George Eliot)	114
Funeral Custom	115
Decking Graves with Flowers	116
A Sprig of Rosemary ("for Remembrance")	116
The Duologues of the Peasantry	117
The Harvest Home	120
A Costume Procession	121
The Candle-Light Auction for Grazing Rights	123
The Payment of Wroth Silver at Knightlow Cross	126
The Stuffed Marrow for Christmas	134
The Roasted Crabs	135
The Thomasing	136
Humphrey How, the good Porter of Stoneleigh Abbey	137
Christmas Carols	138

xiv   *Contents*

The Mumming	*Page* 140
The Yule-Log	141
Elder Wine and Hot Toast for Breakfast on Christmas Morning	142
Carols for the New Year	145
Robert Dover (Director of the Games on Cotswold Hills), a Native of Shakespeare's Greenwood	147

The Folklore   149

The Horse's White Foot	152
The Robin's Song	153
The Sky-Signs	155
The Fleecy Barometer	156
Rain Signs	157
The Bee-Hives	158
Telling the Bees	159
The Swarming of Bees	159
Catching Ascension Day Rain	160
The Oak and the Ash Proverbs	161
The Fern Seed Love Charm	163
Moon Signs	163
The Magpie and Noah's Ark	165
Cheeses and Sneezes	166

Contents

	Page
The Stranger in the Tea-Cup	169
The Spark in the Candle Flame	169
The Stranger on the Grate	170
The Burnt Milk	172
Egg-Shells and Laying Hens	172
The Turkey's Gobble	173
The Tree Cure for Rickets	175
Passing through the Cleft	175
Ring-Finger	177
The Baby's Birthday	178
Lucky Birthdays	179
Death and the Open Door	179
The Sage Tree and the Master	180
The Whistling Woman	181

The Birds and Trees — 183

The Bird's Sanctuary	185
The Proud Tailor	186
"Leafy Leamington"	187
The Holly Walk (where Mr. Carker met Edith Granger)	188
The Town Rooks	188
The Thieving Rook	189
The Throstle	190

The Missel-Thrush	Page 191
The Bullfinch	191
The Bird-Catcher	192
The Ring-Ousel	192
The Landrail	194
The Skylark	196
The Skylark's Flight	196
The Companions of the Rustic	197
The Magpie as Seer and Socialist	198
The Carrion Crow a Thief	200
Jackdaws Building	201
Rooks and Jackdaws at School	202
An Entrance to the Forest of Arden	203
The Prayer at Coughton Cross	203
"The Round Tree" (the Middle of England)	204
Gospel Oaks	206
The Pollard Oak in Stoneleigh Home Park	207
Shakespeare's Oak in Stoneleigh Deer Park	208
The Big Oak at Snitterfield	209
"The Three Ladies" (planted by the Poet Jago's daughter)	210
Shakespeare's Crab-Tree at Bidford	211
The Elms	212

Contents

The Walnuts at George Eliot's "Hall Farm"	*Page* 212
The Big Chestnut at Offchurch Bury (on the Site of the Palace of Offa, the Mercian King)	213

The Parson 215

The Festival on the Green	217
At the Christening of the great Bell, "St. Paul"	217
The Country Parson (Dr. Samuel Parr, LL.D.)	218
The Small Vanities of the Rustics, and the Parson's	219
The Peal of Bells	223
A Letter to a Norwich Friend	223
A Lover of Dancing	226
Macready and Sarah Kemble on the Green	226
The Bowling Green at Leamington	226
The Parson and the Duchess of Bedford in the Country Dance	228
The Parson as Campanologist	229
As a Student of Theocritus, Virgil, and Warwickshire Pastoral Life	230
As an Amateur Gardener	231

xviii *Contents*

    As a Friend of Landor's   *Page* 232
    As Landor's Eulogist   232
    As a Merry-maker at the Easter Lifting   235

The Poets   237

    Shenstone and the Leasowes   239
    At a Warwickshire School   240
    The Meeting with Jago   241
    Jago's Apostrophe to Solihull   242
    Dr. Samuel Johnson nominated for School-
        master at Solihul School   242
    Shenstone at Pembroke College, Oxford   243
    With Jago at Beaudesert Parsonage   243
    Three Poets in Arden—Somerville, Shenstone,
        and Jago   246
    With Lady Luxborough at Barrells, Henley-
        in-Arden   246
    Shenstone's Lines to Lady Luxborough   248
    Her Ladyship's Poetry to Shenstone   249
    Her Letters and Death   250
    "Written at an Inn at Henley"   251
    Death of Somerville (the Poet of "The
        Chase") at Edstone Hall   251
    Shenstone's Poetic Lament for his Friend   252

Contents

Somerville's Epitaph	Page 253
Shenstone's Death at the Leasowes	254
His Burial at Hales-Owen	254
Jago's Poetic Lament for his Friend in his Poem of "Edge Hill"	255
"The Fate of the Leasowes"—Shenstone's finest Poem	256

The Novelist   257

The Way to "Cheverel Manor"	259
The Griff Miner's Ignorance of George Eliot and her Books	260
South Farm (the Birthplace of the Novelist)	265
Arbury Hall	265
The Romance of Charles Brandon, a former Owner	266
Sir Roger Newdigate ("Sir Christopher Cheverel")	272
Gothicising the Hall	273
Robert Evans ("Adam Bede")	275
Scenes of "Mr. Gilfil's Love Story"	276
The Death of Sir Roger Newdigate	278
Griff—George Eliot's Native Village	279

The First Railway in Shakespeare's Greenwood *Page*	280
Mr. Newdigate's Canal	282
To London by Water	283
Chilvers Coten (the "Shepperton" of the Novelist)	284
The Original of "Mr. Gilfil"	285
The Village of Corley and the "Hall Farm" of "Adam Bede"	287
George Eliot, the Novelist-Historian of Shakespeare's Greenwood	288

The Language

The Forest of Arden.—"Hungry Harbury."—The Harbury Carrier.—The Blue *Biggen*.—The *Bravery*.—The *Reckling* and *Dilling*.—The Nesh Child.—The Frem Child.—The Wench.—The Faggot.—The Slummock.—Hedgehog and Urchin.—Terms of Punishment.—*Shog* and *Shogged*.—"Lobbs' Courtship."—A *Shive*.—The T sound for D.—Call: "no call to."—To fend.—"Shakespeare Hall," where the Poet wrote his Sonnets.—Flower Names.—"Naked Ladies."—A *Blench*.—On for of.—The Butty.—To Cumber.—*Moither, Mummock*, or Moil.—The Batlet.—The Dag.—The Anointed Scaramouch.—The Cade Lamb.—"This fore-wearied Flesh."—O for W.—*Wuts*.—The Added N.—Rimming.—*Unked*.—To Favour or Judge.—The Ten Commandments.—The *Deaf-Nut*.—Tooting.—Brevetting.—Othergates.—A Colly Day.—Mortal in Love or Folly: the poetry of the language.—Its close Alliance to the Bible and Shakespeare.

The Language

"*They're cur'ous talkers i' this country, sir; the gentry's hard work to hunderstand 'em. I was brought up among the gentry, sir, an' got the turn o' their tongue when I was a bye. Why, what do you think the folks about here say for 'heven't you?' the gentry, you know, says 'heven't you'—well, the people about here says 'hanna yey.' It's what they call the 'dileck' as is spoke hereabout, sir. That's what I've heard Squire Donnithorne say many a time; 'it's the dileck,' says he.*"

Mr. Casson in "Adam Bede."

Though something less than two and a half hours' journey from London to the fringe of the once famous Forest of Arden in leafy Warwickshire, it is little short of surprising that at the fag end of the nineteenth century, the same forms of speech in vogue in the days of Shakespeare, and even before his days, should still be in use in every part of the county in all the beauty of their quaintness, directness, and simplicity.

I say "surprising," for it really does seem so, that the central county of this Merrie England of ours, the very home and seat of manufactures and therefore the abode of civilisation—since civilisation is the handmaiden of manufactures—and the Mecca to which the teeming millions of the great Western land make a continuous pilgrimage, augmented by the vast phalanx of English-speaking peoples which annually pays a visit to this famous historical and classic county; it is surprising, I say, that in the whole of Warwickshire (in cities and towns as well as in villages and hamlets) may be heard and seen the same idioms, the same pronunciations, and the same methods of spelling as were wont to be observed three and four hundred years ago, when civilisation (if we are to read aright, as we are told to read them, the signs, the shows, and the affectations of this present age) must have been an unborn child, or, if born, merely a puling infant in its swaddling clothes.

It *is* surprising, but I also think it is extremely pleasant ; for civilisation, utterly offended, as it seemed to be, with the picturesque forms of speech migrating from the pastoral plains of the greenwood to the hot-houses of society, invented a language of its own, a catch-word or slang language, which, however " smart" and applicable it may be in the mouths of those who are pleased to use it, cannot compare in grip, in appositeness, or in poetical feeling, with the strong, broad, euphonious, and clearly expressed provincialisms—centuries old as they are, but still in vogue, with an unslayable uniformity of meaning and utterance; and in leafy Warwickshire, owing, perhaps, to the high place which it holds in the best of English literature through the genius of its literary sons and daughters, it *is* pleasant to know that the old forms of speech, so valued and so intrinsically valuable as the original expression of an ancient and historical people, are, probably, as deeply rooted to-day as they were in primeval days.

Why it is so I cannot say. "Leafy Warwickshire" *was* an impenetrable forest. Even in modern times, as Elton tells us in his "Origins of English History," it was so thickly wooded that a squirrel might leap from tree to tree for nearly the whole length of the county; and the character of the country at an earlier period is gathered from the fact that in 1250 the woods were so thick hereabout that the Constable of the Shire was commanded to cut down six acres in breadth between Coventry and Warwick for the better security of foot passengers; so under those circumstances it is no marvel that the language of the hardy woodlanders should not have suffered much from the inroads of Court gallants.

But Warwickshire, though still leafy, though still, with regard to some of its villages and hamlets at least, perfectly isolated from the world of fashionable language, is far from being impenetrable to-day. The railways of the nineteenth century, following in the footsteps of the medieval Constable of the Shire, have cut their way in a network of lines right through the heart of "The Heart of England." The iron metals wind their tortuous route almost up to the doors of Bilton House, near Rugby, where, in the old-time seclusion of the grounds, Addison strolled in his famous "Walk," and where, to this day (at the side of the Walk) towers the magnificent Cedar of Cyprus which tradition says he planted. There is even a railway now constructed from the quaint village of Henley-in-Arden to the equally quaint town of Stratford-on-Avon, through a region of woodland until recently unopened.

Moreover, from the most isolated of the villages, from Wilnecote in the hardy north, to Tysoe (where a fearful instance of the survival of witchcraft occurred in 1875) and Long Compton in the extreme south, the carrier comes almost daily into the fashionable places of modern civilisation; yet with all these links to connect rural with urban life, the phraseology of four hundred years ago remains fixed and unalterable—being handed down, like a family heirloom, from parent to children along the line of generations.

Whether the retention among Warwickshire people of the dialect form of speech is regarded by them as a sacred trust, whether it is employed and retained unconsciously, or whether as modern superstition has hinted, there is witchcraft in it, it certainly is a very curious fact that country-bred folk in Shakespeare's greenwood, no matter how long they may have left their cottages on the heath, in a coomb, or by the side of a woodlet, or how busily they may have engaged in urban affairs, never entirely lose their native dialect.

As an illustration of the inability of country-born folk in Warwickshire to cast off the yoke (or to put it more felicitously, the yoke which they do not seem to want to cast off) of their natural language, even though their contact with town is busy, daily, and continuous, I may instance the case of the Harbury carrier.

Now Harbury is a village but six miles south-east of the fashionable town of Leamington, where there is a college of some eminence, High Schools for girls, preparatory Academies innumerable, and so many scholastic institutions, all racing towards a perfect erudition in everything, that language ought to be in an extremely forward state in that "Seat of Learning" as Leamington has been called.

The village of Harbury rejoices in the prefix of Hungry, though with quite a different meaning from the "Hungry Grafton" of the Shakespearean doggerel; the definition of "Hungry Harbury" being a storehouse for grain, four windmills having existed there in past times, whereas "Hungry Grafton" is the signification for barren, waste, and unfertile land—literally land that is hungry.

Harbury was also the scene of the ministry of the Reverend Richard Jago (born at Beaudesert in the heart of the Forest of Arden on October 1, 1715, and died at Snitterfield on May 8, 1781), the poet of "Edge Hill," who in "The Diary of Expenses," found among his manuscripts at his death, uses that good old Warwickshire word *strike* for bushel, a word as frequently heard to-day as it was used frequently by the Lady Jane Verney in the "Compton Verney Accounts," kept by her ladyship in the eighteenth century and still honoured by use at Compton Verney, Kineton, and the neighbouring villages and townships.

As I am anxious to make this account of the language of Shakespeare's greenwood as interesting as I can, in the hope that it may serve as a contribution to the rural dialect of this charming county which has already been garnered up in the plays of Shakespeare, the novels of George Eliot, and the archives of dialect societies, I shall give the language of the peasants of Warwickshire as I have heard it spoken by them during the past five or six years in the villages near my home at Leamington, premising that in this form—catching the words as they fell from the lips of the rustics—greater value may attach to it, though the words will not necessarily run in the alphabetical order of the dictionary, my object being to write an interesting and chatty account of some of the dialect words of the Warwickshire peasantry, rather than a learned, dry analytical treatise on provincialisms.

The Harbury carrier, then, comes into my " seat of learning " at least three times a week and mingles with the townspeople (who pride themselves upon being what is called "up-to-date"), and yet from that man's speech he might well have been own brother to William, the lover of Audrey, resident in the Forest of Arden in the days when the banished Duke held his Court under the greenwood tree.

"My ould man," he said, meaning his buxom wife younger than himself, whom he sometimes brought with him in the cart, "hev med a blue biggen for the recklin' yander" (a young child was sitting in the conveyance). "'Tis a nesh 'un, ye see, an' canna goo in closen wi' outen summat's on yed when the dag's a-fallin'."

A *biggen* is a dainty little cap worn upon the head of a small infant or young child to keep it from taking cold. In older times the Warwickshire mothers took an especial pride in making these little *biggens*, and some of them (one I have seen dating from the early years of the present century) with their frills, tucks, cords, and edgings were perfect gems of the needlework art. In the Second Part of "King Henry the

Fourth" (Act IV. scene 4), Shakespeare alludes to them in the words:

"*Whose brow with homely biggen bound,*"

clearly indicating the fact that the *biggen* was a home-made article of headdress provided for the *recklin* of the family, or a *nesh* child.

In such *bravery* too is the pretty sentence you may often hear fall from the lips of a Warwickshire peasant woman, standing beneath the honeysuckle of her own door. It refers to a girl's finery, her feathers, flowers, ribbons, and laces, and when, as is usually the case, its utterance is accompanied by a smile, it conveys the sweetest touch of encouragement with the faintest sound of reproach, for the *bravery* of the village fair, matrons as well as maidens, is one of their chief characteristics.

"Eh! Loo, lass," will cry a fond mother of forty, "when I see thee dorned out i' that bravery, it meks me think o' the time when I danced the reel at the Thomasin', an' danced off wi' thy feyther's heart at the same time."

This word as applied to the small fineries of the toilet was evidently in popular use in Shakespeare's days, for he uses it in " The Taming of the Shrew " (Act IV. scene 3); and to-day throughout the Woodland and Feldon of Warwickshire, north and south of the Avon, the same pretty word is constantly heard tripping off the rustic's tongue.

The *reckling* spoken of by the Harbury carrier is, generally speaking, the youngest of the children; it is also applied to the weakest child, or the one longest in growing. This word, with the " g " always dropped (which is a characteristic of Warwickshire rural dialect in all words ending with " ing "), is somewhat extensively used in sequestered villages. It is also spelt " wreckling," though the " w " is more frequently deleted, indicating probably that the child being small and puny is the " reck " or " wreck " of the family in a physical sense.

In some villages nearer the towns a variant of this word is constantly heard. *Dilling* is used instead of " reckling " and has precisely the same significance. For example, a mother at Chilver's Coten, the " Shepperton " of George Eliot, once said within my hearing, "Eh! my baby's the dillin'; she's been a nesh 'un from her birth forrard till now."

Dilling is also applied indiscriminately to all small, long-growing, dwindling things. You cannot go into a farmyard or under the thatch of a cottage in rural Warwickshire without hearing this word. It is in the mouths of farmer, housewife, shepherd, poultry-maid, and child. Every small thing is a *dillin'*. The smallest chicken in the brood is a *dilling*, so are the smallest duckling and gosling; and the *dilling* of the pig's litter is always the object of the housewife's especial care. There is luck in the pig's *dilling*. It is reared up by the bottle, kept in a stuff-lined basket near the kitchen fire, and as much attention paid to it as if it were the *dilling* of the human family.

A *nesh* child is a term which has a meaning almost identical with *reckling* and *dilling* though there is much more pathos in it. It is applied to the suffering side of nature. Anything of whatever age, condition, or calling that is weak, feeble, or ailing is a *nesh* thing. A delicate girl or boy in the mouth of every Warwickshire village housewife, is spoken of as "a *nesh* 'un," and it is quite a usual thing to hear such sentences as "My poor gel's too nesh to goo slummokin' an' trapesin' over fields an' such places as if her were as frem as frem," or "The lovin' laddie's that nesh he canna pump a bucket o' warter wi' outen fetchin's breath as 'ard as smithy bellows."

Now in the Warwickshire rustic's mouth there is a word, which, in direct opposition to *nesh* is often spoken with it, and comes very trippingly from the tongue. I have not noticed it in Shakespeare's plays, but it is firmly rooted in the vocabulary of the peasant in all the little villages of Shakespeare's greenwood, and may very well have been heard in the mouth of Mary Arden in speaking of her son, William. Indeed, it was, and is, the joy of every Warwickshire village mother's heart to be able to call her offspring a *frem* child or *frem* children.

To be *frem* is to be bonnie, lively, healthful, plump, and thriving, and as the bulk of village children are of this order, the word *frem* is in constant use. At Bidford (the "drunken" of the well-known verse) a mother may often be heard cooing to her neighbour as she watches her child playing on the green. "Hey! my lassie be as frem as frem—as frem as the grass yander. I thank God as her be frem. I canna look on a nesh gel wi' outen feelin' sorrerful like. That I canna."

Frem is also used with reference to the natural growths of the earth. Thus luxuriant grass is *frem* grass, well-growing crops are "fine an *frem*," and "the yarbs in your gardin, Mrs. Bycroft, be as frem as ever I seed." The waggoner will call his horse a "*frem* horse"; the shepherd's calves and lambs are "the *fremmest* as he's ever 'ad"; and the young collie is as *frem* a dog as you'd find anywhere. In short, *frem* is the word for anything and everything that is strong, lusty, plump, thriving, and throbbing with health.

Totty Poyser was a *frem* child, yet we find Mrs. Poyser saying in "Adam Bede" (page 123), "Totty, be a good dilling, an' go to sleep now," which seems to indicate that such words as *reckling*, *dilling*, *nesh*, and *frem* are used by Warwickshire mothers sometimes as terms of endearment, and not always with a slavish regard to their original meaning.

As a term of endearment, however, there is perhaps no word of dialect so old and yet so extensively used in the whole of leafy Warwickshire as the word *wench* when applied to a young maid. Since Shakespeare used it in an affectionate sense in "The Taming of the Shrew" (Act V. scene 2), in the fifth Act of "Othello," and again in "Romeo and Juliet" (Act II. scene 4), where Mercutio says:

> "*Alas, poor Romeo! he is already dead;*
> *Stabbed with a white wench's black eye,*

the word *wench* has become as familiar in the pastoral mouth as the speaker's own tongue. And not only in the pastoral mouth, either; for in the mouth of the urban dweller in Warwickshire, "my dear *wench*" is a term constantly heard and approved of by the lucky maiden, who, in the time of dearth, has had the good fortune to win a young man to her side.

And not only is *wench* used by the

rustic sweetheart of leafy Warwickshire as a word of affection to the girl of his choice, but the fond mother trips it off her tongue with the greatest freedom. "Eh! my wench," she says to her daughter, "thee mun be a good gel, an' then ye shall goo to Warwick stattis an' see the wenches 'ired," or "I donna know how 'tis, but thee hanna raggled to be such a good wench as ye was afore you went to Brookington. I do love thee like, my dear wench, an' I do 'ope thee'll be a comfort to me an' thy feyther."

The word *wench* is also employed extensively in an endearing sense by those who have charge of cattle. A favourite cow, mare, ewe, or bitch is always "a *wench*." A pat on the back, and "Eh! she be a good old wench" are sounds of the greatest familiarity in rural Warwickshire.

Then, as is often the case with dialect words, *wench* has a bad side to its character; it is sometimes used as a term of reproach. This is not very frequent, but when it is applied to a girl in this sense, it seems to have an overwhelming feeling of shame attached to it. I have seen a rustic maid cry bitterly at being called a *wench* in that peculiar tone of voice which implies a lightness and looseness of conduct quite inconsistent with the behaviour which should characterise a demure, decorous, and modest girl; while, on the other hand, I have seen the same girl smile radiantly when called a *wench* by her sweetheart or mother. It is, I suppose, all a matter of method. It is the way in which the word is uttered which seems to convey so much to those to whom it is applied.

In its reproachful sense the word *wench* means a bad, loose, vulgar, lewd, riotous woman or girl, who stands upon no ceremony and has no respect for herself or for what her neighbours may think of her. It is thus allied to such peculiarly Warwickshire dialect words of opprobrium as *faggot*, *doxy*, *hussy*, *slummock*, and *slat*. All these words are of venerable age, and are in constant use to-day in all the villages of Shakespeare's greenwood. *Doxy* has, perhaps, the worst signification. Shakespeare himself uses the word in "A Winter's Tale" (Act IV. scene 2), and the meaning it had then (that "a *doxy*" was neither maid, wife, nor widow) is the same which it has now; with the addition that a gaily dressed woman or girl is sometimes called "a *doxy*" independently of her ethical position—for example, "Eh! what a fine doxy Moll hev become."

A *faggot* has not precisely the same meaning among Warwickshire rustics as *doxy*, though it is somewhat akin in signification. It is a term which does not imply quite so much as *doxy*, and yet sufficient to make the ears of a maid tingle who has any respect for herself. If one girl calls another a *faggot* it not infrequently leads to a measurement of each other's hair. A *faggot* literally means a careless, good-for-nothing, untidy person; and as the majority of Warwickshire girls and women are noted for their neat appearance and thrifty, careful manners, it may easily be imagined how heartily they resent such a term of reproach as *faggot*.

That there are *some* careless, untidy Warwickshire lasses, however, must be true, otherwise the word *slummock* would not be so often heard in passing through the villages of Shakespeare's greenwood. "Come thee here, you slummock," cries an indignant mother, spying her child with frock unfastened, pinafore untied, or hat slouched on head. Any loosely attired, slatternly person (man, woman, or child) is a *slummock*. You may not uncommonly hear a man saying, "Donna thee look at me, Mister; I be such a slummock. I hanna 'ad time to goo an' tidy mesen, yet like."

A ragged colt is a *slummockin'* creature, so is a moulting fowl; anything, in fine, which has not an air of trimness and neatness about it is a *slummock*. It is a word which expresses much, and is very closely allied to that other reproachful word, *moikin*, which literally means a scarecrow, but which is quite as often applied to persons who are negligent in their personal appearance as to the effigy which scares crows.

There is another term of reproach very frequently used in Warwickshire villages, but this is directed by the fair sex against the sterner one, and chiefly against boys. It is not a very pretty word, though an important one in the dialect phraseology of this greenwood by reason of its age and Shakespearean association.

"If thee donna come in, ye hedgehog, I'll lace thee warmly."

This is an expression I heard issuing from the mouth of a buxom woman, with well-oiled and well-combed hair, who was standing at the door of a thatched cottage in the village of Offchurch—one of the Warwickshire seats of the Earls of Aylesford. On a patch of green pasture in front of the cottage an untidy boy (presumably her son) was idly stretched out playing with a young lurcher dog and showing no disposition to obey the parental command.

Now *hedgehog*, as a term of reproach, has been in vogue in rural Warwickshire for a period of at least three hundred years. It is used by Shakespeare in "Richard the Third," when the ex-Queen, Margaret, in cursing Richard, Duke of Gloster, calls him a *hedgehog*. In this greenwood the *hedgehog* is also known as an *urchin*, and in former times, as is set down in many parish books in the immediate vicinity of Stratford-on-Avon, there were so many *hedgehogs* or *urchins* overrunning the land that sixpence a head was given for every one brought to the farmer or churchwardens—the latter entering the payments in the official accounts.

This offer of reward brought both pleasure and profit to those concerned, and in it, I think, is to be traced the association which has given to boys, from Shakespeare's days to the present, the undesirable names of *hedgehog* and *urchin*. Shakespeare himself alludes to the *urchin* in "Titus Andronicus" (Act II. scene 3).

The *lace* mentioned in the above sentence has a peculiar meaning in the lingo of the Warwickshire peasant. It literally means to beat or thrash. When a mother or father say to their son for some committed offence, "You mark, my laddie, I'll lace thee for that," they mean, "I'll beat you for that; I'll thrash you for it." There are several words in the same category, and they are all extensively used. For example, such expressions as "I'll warm you," "I'll leather you when ye come 'ome," "I'll thrape ye warmly," are quite familiar in the mouths of rustic humanity, and although they have not the signet stamp of Shakespeare upon them, as scores of Warwickshire words have, they are very expressive dialect terms, and are perfectly well understood by the children, who know that, though the words vary in sound and spelling, yet they all have warmth in them.

Talking one morning to the shepherd of the Coomb Farm at Lillington, about a mile and a half from my home at Leamington, he suddenly surprised me by saying, "Well, I mun shog on a bit. I were up at four, ye know, an' I can welly do wi' a shive o' summat to et an' a tot o' tay." Here was a perfect professor of Warwickshire dialect—a veritable Shakespearean peasant in the art of the mother tongue! "Shog on a bit. A shive o' summat an' a tot o' tay." It was quite pleasant to hear this old son of Abel tripping out freshly and freely words which Shakespeare had used three centuries ago.

To *shog* is a word very much used at the present time by the peasants of this delightful county. Whether it is older than "jog" I cannot say, but as Shakespeare mentions *shog* in "Henry the Fifth" (Act II. scene 3), we are entitled to regard it as a dialect word of some importance. It means to jog off, to make off, to move on slowly and easily, to shamble, to sidle.

Some time ago I rescued from the memory of a farmer at the village of Southam, near Rugby, a quaintly humorous old Warwickshire ballad called "Lobb's Courtship." It deals with the love affairs of one Lobb, who has fixed his attentions upon a bright country maid, Nell, whom, after he has opened the ball by sending her two ripe apples and a letter, he gaily goes to court. The ballad, as given to me orally, then proceeds :

> *The cows were all turned out to grass,*
> *As Lobb set off to see his lass;*
> *He oiled his shoes and combed his hair*
> *Like one a-going to a fair.*
> *His stick was bended like a bow ;*
> *His handkerchief it made a show ;*
> *His hat stood like a pot-lid round ;*
> *His coat was of the fustian browned ;*
> *And so he went and Nell he found.*
>
> *" Dear Nellie, how dost do ?" says he,*
> *" Oh ! will you come along with me,*
> *O'er yander close to yander stile ?"*
> *" Indeed," says Nell, " I can't awhile."*
> *So Nell steps in and shuts the door,*
> *And Lobb* shogged *off and said no more.*

It will thus be observed that *shog* and *shogged*, as Warwickshire dialect words, have had a certain dignity shown to them by the poets, ancient and modern, which gives them additional importance in the vocabulary of original country expressions, apart from the weight of their age and the fact that they are in use to-day, as familiarly in the peasant's mouth as in the days of the great Warwickshire poet.

A *shive* has also the garments of antiquity upon it, blended with the dress of modern days. If you go to-day into a Warwickshire hay- or corn-field when the labourers are having their lunch or dinner, the word *shive* will often salute the ear. " I mun hev a shive o' bread and bacon," says the driver of the cutting-machine, getting out his knife and opening it. " I can do wi' a shive, too," chimes in the man wi' the rake, producing his parcel of food from a flag basket. A *shive* means a shave, a slice, a piece. Shakespeare caught the meaning of *shive* to a nicety in " Titus Andronicus " (Act II. scene 1) where he says :

*What, man! more water glideth by the mill
Than wots the miller of; and easy it is
Of a cut loaf to steal a* shive.

A saying with a meaning exactly identical with Shakespeare's simile is still current in the cottage homes of rural Warwickshire, where many housewives, full of generosity and very hospitable as they always are, encourage a guest to eat by saying, " Now, donna thee spare ; a slice off on a cut loaf be never missed." A *shive* is sometimes substituted by them for slice ; but the men, as a rule, use the word *shive* more frequently than the women, and especially when they are out in the fields cutting their food with a pocket-knife.

The word *tot* used by the coomb shepherd is a word very prevalent in all parts of rural Warwickshire. It means a cup, a mug, a saucerful, or a drop of tea, or anything to drink. " Come thee in now, Biddy, lass, an' hev a tot o' cider," or " Hey, I be so dry like, I could just do wi' a tot o' drink," are expressions commonly heard in the fields and lanes. *Tot* has also a different signification when used in conjunction with " out " or " up." To " tot out " means to pour out.

In the snug parlour of a wayside inn in leafy Warwickshire *tot* in this sense is an extremely familiar word. " Now Andrey, lad, tot out," one tippler will say to another, meaning him to pour out. Again, *tot* is used in a slightly varied form as " Come, butty, tot up," which means to drink up. The landlord of the inn, too, is often requested to " tot up " the score set down to a customer, meaning to add it up to find out how much is owing.

The Warwickshire peasant is occasionally prone to the use of " t " and " th " instead of " d " in some of his words, with an effect at once peculiar and amusing to the town-bred man. One day in walking over the fields from Leamington to Lillington (the latter a village which seems to have had more than ordinary interest for Nathaniel Hawthorne when he was a sojourner at Leamington in the 'fifties) I encountered a man upon a stile looking intently over the red roofs and yellow rick ends of this Warwickshire "Sweet Auburn." He appeared travel worn and was about the last person from whose mouth I should have expected to hear snatches of good dialect, and yet no sooner had I reached the stile than he said, without a word of introduction :

"There usen to be a lather over the runnel yander when I was a kiddie. Mother was nigh afraid to trusten me as far as thisen, but I crossed the lather to t'other side as aim as aim."

A *lather*, in the language of the dwellers in Shakespeare's greenwood, means a ladder, or little bridge with spars. This word is not very common, but is still used by the older inhabitants of the village who have not had the advantages of a course of University Extension Lectures. "Goo an' fatch me that lather theer by the rickyard yon," is a sentence which may be occasionally heard coming from the tongue of the thatcher.

The word *call* is perhaps one of the most frequently used in the whole of Warwickshire dialect words. It means cause or reason. You cannot go into any cottage home in any of the villages and get into conversation with the peasants without hearing *call* repeated over and over again. The word must have been as largely in use in George Eliot's younger days as it is at the present time, for it is constantly to be found in the dialect of all her Warwickshire books. One example will suffice to show the significance of *call*. It is to be found in " Silas Marner " (p. 109), where Silas and Dolly Winthorpe are speaking about naming the child which has come so unexpectedly to the weaver's hearthstone. Silas has suggested " Hephzibah," but Dolly thinks that a hard name.

" It's a Bible name," said Silas, old ideas recurring.

" Then I've no *call* to speak again it," said Dolly.

In speaking of Silas Marner and Eppie, it may be useful at this point to allude to another familiar dialect word, in extensive vogue in Warwickshire at the present day, which George Eliot puts into the mouth of Eppie. It is that scene in which Godfrey Cass comes to the weaver's house to claim his long unacknowledged child. Eppie is unwilling to leave Silas, and says, with unaffected simplicity : " I can't feel as I've got any father but one. I've always thought of a little home where he'd sit i' the corner, and I should fend and do everything for him ; I can't think o' no other home."

To *fend*, in the language of the country-folk of Shakespeare's greenwood, is to work, and Eppie's meaning was that she would like to work for Silas, her real, though not legal, father. It is a word very often in the mouths of parents when their children have made them angry. "I shanna stan' much more o' this, I can tell thee. Thee'lt hev to goo an' fend for thysen," a father will say to his son. A mother will also say to her daughter in the kindest manner: "Ah! me wench, when the time comes for thee to fend for theesen, 'tis then ye'll find out what life be i' this warld. *I* had to goo an' fend for mysen before I was nigh thy age."

As a dialect word, *fend* is also common among the urban working folk of Staffordshire, but, so far as I have been able to gather, it is only used in the rural districts of Warwickshire, and there quite frequently.

The tenacity with which dialect words connected with wayside flowers and plants in Warwickshire cling to life is certainly one of the most interesting features in a subject fraught with interest. Shakespeare, we know, was a dear lover of flowers, chiefly wild flowers, and mentions many of them in his plays by the local names they were known by in his day. In connection with the poet's love of flowers there is a curious floral fact which may be aptly mentioned here, though it has no reference to the dialect of the county.

Between the celebrated Wroxall Abbey, near Warwick (once the residence of Sir Christopher Wren), and the unique moated house of Baddesley Clinton, near Knowle, there is an old house which for many years belonged to the Shakespeare family. It is a timber-framed structure, built, like Charlecote Hall, the home of the Lucys, in the shape of the letter E, so prevalent in the reign of Queen Elizabeth, and so formed out of compliment to her. In a little room over the porch Shakespeare is said to have written his sonnets; and it is shrewdly surmised that, as the name of Isabella Shakespeare appears in the register as Matron or Superioress of one of the religious houses in the neighbourhood, this is the ideal Forest of Arden depicted in "Measure for Measure." The remnant of the Forest comes close up to this old homestead, and is known as "the High Wood." Near to it, strange to say, the lily of the valley grows wild, yet it is one of the few plants which Shakespeare does not mention.

In going down the Warwickshire lanes, those isolated from the public way, children may be seen gathering the flowers of that umbelliferous plant, the hemlock, which is very common in the hedges and ditches here, and grows several feet in height. The children call the hemlock "keck," and you may often hear them saying to one another, "Let's goo and gather a bunch o' keck." I have known the hemlock as "keck" since my childhood and Shakespeare knew it by the same name in his boyhood. He mentions it in "Henry the Fifth" (Act V. scene 2).

Then there is his pleasant allusion in "Love's Labour's Lost" (Act V. scene 2) to the flower which he calls "lady smocks," but which many Warwickshire peasant folk call "smell smocks" by that curious rule of contrariety which sometimes distinguishes them, for "smell smocks" have no smell in them.

When daisies pied and violets blue,
  And lady-smocks all silver white,
  And cuckoo buds of yellow hue,
    Do paint the meadows with delight.

These flowers so delicate, fragile, and quickly shedding, grow in prodigious numbers in the pastures of leafy Warwickshire. "Cum an' cull a nosegay o' smell smocks" is quite a familiar saying among the children, and the mothers, when they come home, will greet them with the words, "Hey, thee hev gotten a dandy bunch o' smell smocks, my gel. Wheer didst raggle to get they?"

Perhaps the "lords and ladies" are as popular a floral emblem among the rustic children as anything in the flora of Warwickshire. They are, of course, the wild arum, which in April and May everywhere adorns the ditches and hedge bottoms of this delightful country. When they are not "lords and ladies" they are "cows and calves" in the phraseology of the peasant children, and when they are not "cows and calves" they are sometimes "bulls and cows"— most curious names, it must be owned, for such pleasant plants, and words of which the origin does not seem to be known.

There is one other curious local name for a plant which should be mentioned here. Allusion is made to the common meadow saffron. In the leas at Castle Bromwich, near the flourishing city of Birmingham, this plant was wont to grow in large numbers in the beginning of September. The country people call these pretty, though poisonous flowers "naked ladies," because they come up without any leaves. They also apply the same name indiscriminately to any plant which has flowers on naked scapes, appearing at different times from the leaves.

In the core of Nature's heart words that come "trippingly from the tongue," as Hamlet would say, are those most in use with the rustic. A desire for condensation and abbreviation is also apparent. The peasant will say "Adone, will ye," meaning "have done," thus merging two English words into one. When Audrey or Phyllis are troubled with love affairs the fond mother will say, "Hey, lassie, adone wi't, or

I shanna catch a blench on thy bonnie eye no ways. Now do adone."

A *blench* is a word conveying an enigma to the townsman in the sense in which the rustic of Shakespeare's greenwood uses it. To the townsman a *blench* would seem to imply a sudden whitening or paleness of the countenance, as a blenching of the face. In the dialect of the Warwickshire peasant it has a totally different signification; a meaning, indeed, at once pretty, endearing, and poetical. A *blench* means a glimpse, a glance, a look. A greenwood maiden, gives her lover a *blench* on her bonnie eye, a gamekeeper catches a *blench* or a glimpse of the poacher setting his snares in forbidden preserves, and a Grandfer William takes "a good *blench*," a good look, at the smart coaching party driving gaily through his Sleepy Hollow.

In the word "on" used in place of "of" we catch what may be called a *blench* of Shakespeare's application of his homely mother-tongue.

We are such stuff
As dreams are made on,

says the immortal Warwickshire poet in "The Tempest" (Act IV. scene 1), and in three centuries and more since the date of that play the peasant of Shakespeare's greenwood may be heard saying, "That dream as I telled thee on as my butty had," or "A man as I knows on." It is always *on* and never *of*, and if the truth must be told it really does give a picturesque touch to the sentence.

That *on* is like the ancient village pewter pot, it has been handed down without a break for centuries, and is now as much alive as the bricks spoken of in the Second Part of "King Henry the Sixth" (Act IV. scene 2). "Sir, he made a chimney in my father's house, and the bricks are alive at this day to testify to it."

In the language of the isolated dwellers in these solitary nooks of Nature there are sundry dialect words used in a fondling and companionable sense. The word *wench*, alluded to in an earlier portion of this sketch, is one of them. That is applied distinctively to females of whatever kind, calling, condition, or rank. In a similar sense the word used towards males is *butty*. It means a friend, a companion, a mate, and sometimes something more; for it is not infrequently that a village lass will, in a merry mood, call her sweetheart her *butty*. Strictly, however, the word is the property of the males. It is used both to human and animal friends. The poacher's human companion on his nightly prowls is always his *butty*, and the shepherd will address his dog something after this fashion: "Hey, bless his four paws; he's a dear old butty, aye, an' a goodly."

It has been said that the language of the Warwickshire greenwood is more akin to the language of Shakespeare and the English Bible than any other English dialect. Certainly it has the completeness, the simplicity, the directness, and the force of both the Bible and Shakespeare. This fact can well be seen in the word *cumber*, so frequently heard in the mouth of the Warwickshire peasant. "Hey, the cumber that I had wi' that lad," cries the mother in despair for the well-being of her son. *Cumber* means trouble, burden, weight, care. George Eliot alludes to it in "Adam Bede" (chap. xxvi. p. 241) where Lisbeth speaks to her son Adam : "I know 'tis a grit honour for thee to be so looked on, an' whose to be prouder on it nor thy mother? Hadna' she the cumber o' rearin' thee an' doin' for thee all these years?"

In the scriptural story of the barren fig-tree the meaning of *cumber* is precisely the same as its significance to-day. The fig-tree cumbered the ground, in other words troubled and burdened the ground with a great care, like the rearing of children, which, in the opinion of some Warwickshire housewives and mothers, is a thankless and barren office.

Other words there are in constant vogue of a kindred meaning. One of these is *moither*. No peasant in a certain condition of mind ever fails to make use of this word. It is one of those that come trippingly from the tongue. "Adone, I tell ye, ye moither me to death," cries the mother to the hardy rustic lad who persists in importuning for a holiday. To *moither* is to worry, to bother, to bewilder. This word is indigenous to the soil of urban as well as rural Warwickshire, and it may even be heard in the mouth of a fair huntress rebuking her horse with the words, "Be quiet, sir, and don't moither me so."

Mummock is a curious word in the same category. A baby *mummocks* its mother, that is pulls her about, worries her. Often in the silence of these leafy lanes the voice of the rustic may be heard screaming through a cottage door in far from dulcet or kindly tones, "Adone, ye lil mummock, ye moither me above a bit." In another sense *mummock* expresses sorrow and mourning, as "I shall mummock mesel' into me grave when thee art gone." The nightingale mummocks or mourns for the eggs of which she has been robbed, and so on. As an expression of sorrow *mummock* is used throughout the range of living things whether of the human, brute, or bird creation.

To continue the set of words denoting worry or expressing sorrow, I may instance the truly Shakespearean word *moil*. No single word in the dialect of the Warwickshire rustic is, perhaps, more expressive than this. It is upon the tongue of every man, woman, and child. "The moil o' this life pulls me down to the ground," sighs the weary villager, and the sentence clearly brings out the meaning of the word. *Moil*, in its practical sense, is but another name for toil. It simply means labour, hard work, drudgery, care and trouble, and very forcibly emphasises the jeremiad of Job, "Man is born unto trouble as the sparks fly upward." In the Warwickshire fields and lanes you may hear this word *moil* more frequently than any other. It is applied in many ways. The young lambs *moil* their mothers; the sciatica in the joints of the rustic greybeard "moils him terrible"; and the young lass is sadly *moiled* because her lover will not come to the point of proposing.

Girt in his own native greenwood and rarely visiting the scenes where men most do congregate (except, perhaps, the Stratford-on-Avon or Warwick pleasure fairs held in October of the year), the Warwickshire rustic keeps to the old manners and ancient tongue as rigidly as were kept the laws of the Medes and Persians. The tongue of Shakespeare is, in many ways, the peasant's own tongue, and no more fitting honour could be done to the world's poet than to use the language in which he spoke and wrote.

In the course of her laundry work the Warwickshire housewives may frequently be heard calling out, "Hey, but you mun give me the batlet; I canna do withouten she." Now the word *batlet* is direct from Shakespeare's time. In "As You Like It" (Act II. scene 4) Touchstone says: "And I remember the kissing of her batlet"—the *batlet* that the pleasing Jane Smile had used in her washing.

The *batlet* of Shakespeare is the "dolly" of the modern housewife—a wooden machine or bat for beating or dollying the house linen. It was also known as "the maiden," by which name it is dignified to-day by many of the homely women of the Warwickshire greenwood. "Come, bring me the maiden;" "I mun hev the batlet;" "Wheer's the dolly?" are terms in everyday use, and are clearly indicative of the hold which Shakespeare's tongue has upon the rustics of his own greenwood.

A townsman going down some of the

more isolated lanes in the evening of the day may often hear a parent calling to her child, "Come in, little dillin', the dag's fallin' on thee, an' thee'rt no hat on thy yed." Now that word *dag* is one of the picturesque peculiarities of the Warwickshire rustic dialect. It means dew, moisture, or fine rain. The old weather-worn shepherd is anxious to in-barn his young eanlings "afore the dag comes on"; the watchful mother both morning and evening will place a biggen or cap upon the head of her youngest born "to keep the dag off on ye." My old friend, Shepherd Amos, of the Coomb Farm, has often addressed to me the words, "It be as heavy a dag, sir, this marnin' as I 'ood wish to see afore Martimas Day, so it be." Though some peasants do say dew the majority invariably use the word *dag*.

Perhaps there are more really curious, and withal interesting, words uttered in Shakespeare's greenwood than in the greenwood of any other county, and as I have stated above, the apparent kinship of some of these words with words to be found in the English Bible, is not a little remarkable. As an example of this, instance may be made of the word *anointed*. The peculiar significance of the word lies in the fact that it has an evil rather than a good interpretation. The Warwickshire rustic boy who has incurred the displeasure of an elder is "an anointed young scaramouch, folly-fit for Old Harry"; that is to say, the lad is *anointed* with the oil of wickedness, is, in fact, a very wicked boy indeed.*

So glib has this word become in the mouth of the peasant that everybody or everything that has done what is considered to be wrong is assailed with the word *anointed*. The liberty-loving lass who, in spite of her mother's expressed veto, goes to Warwick hiring fair, is, when she comes home, an "anointed bad gel"; the waggoner's horse which will not go fast enough to please the driver is an "anointed ould slow-coach"; and the cow that kicks over the milk bucket is called an "anointed old jade."

In another and more endearing sense is to

* In *Folk-Lore*, vol. ii. pp. 188–189, Mr. Poulton explains the term by reference to the seventeenth-century sect of the *Anointers* mentioned in Plot's "Oxfordshire."

be noted the epithet *cade*. This is a well-known Warwickshire word, peculiar, I believe, to Shakespeare's greenwood and its borders, where so many terms of dialect have their origin and their permanent habitation. *Cade* is the rustic's pet name for anything that is tame, mild, or gentle. The lamb, for example, that has been reared in the homestead by bottle, through the loss of its dam, is "as cade as cade," that is to say, as tame and gentle as could be. When the colt has been rough-ridden and broken to harness, then "she be cade enough." Everything that is meek and mild in bird or beast is "a cade thing." The term is also used by the young men to their lasses. Whenever a rustic damsel is more than usually gentle or dainty she is called "a pretty cade Jill."

I have heard the dialect of the Warwickshire peasant spoken of as being "very broad." Certainly there are words in the tongue which might come within the range of that definition, but they are in a minority. When you meet a jaded peasant woman in a narrow lane—a "chewer" as she would call it—resting upon what has, perhaps, been a hard journey, and she tells you she is "fore-wearied wi' her jaunt," I think you may say that the language is poetical.

To be *fore-wearied* is to be very tired—in fact quite dead beat. The term is much in use with the grandams and grandfers of the villages, though it may be heard now and then tripping from the tongue of a youthful wight who ought not to know what it is to be physically *fore-wearied*. Such a son of his shire as Shakespeare was could not well miss this poetical term, and accordingly in "King John" (Act II. scene 1) he speaks of "this fore-wearied flesh."

One of the "broad" uses of the mother tongue as illustrated by the peasant of Shakespeare's greenwood is the sounding of the letter "o" as if it were "w." This truly is a broad and curious characteristic and really somewhat grates upon the ear of those in search of expressive and picturesque language. The harvester I meet near the Red House Farm at Lillington astonished me one hot day by saying, "Hey, the weather's uncommon—uncommon it be. The wuts be amost ready for the blades now." Oats are *wuts* in the dialect of the Warwickshire peasant; and in this and similar uses of the "w" for "o" he betrays the one touch of broadness which is the single blemish upon his plain, direct, and picturesque language.

A similar perversion of the letters of the alphabet is to be seen in the substitution of "y" for "h" or "i." This, too, has a striking effect, as any one who has been much among the Warwickshire rustics can readily testify. To hear a man who has been accidentally struck on the head by a fellow worker crying out, "Come, butty, my yed yent 'ard enough for that sort o' game, ye know," when he means that his "head is not," is very quaint and amusing indeed. Nearly every rustic, devoted to his own rood of earth or migrating "to fresh woods and pastures new," uses the word *yent* for "is not." With him, too, are such pronounced peculiarities of speech as *wevver* for however, and *yarbs* for herbs; as "Ye hev a good bed o' yabs theer, yent ye?" In this sense *yent* stands for haven't or have not.

In the Vale of the Red Horse somewhere about Michaelmas Day sundry farm waggons may be seen at intervals piled high with articles of domestic furniture with the rustic children seated upon the top. These are the belongings of the hired labourer whose term of service being ended at one farm is removing to another. If the peasant walking at the horse's head be questioned as to his journey at so early an hour in the morning he will say, "We be rimmin' to Tysoe, sir. Our turn's done at Radway, an' we'm obliged to get off on the ground afore the dag's dry."

This word *rimming* is very picturesque—almost as much so as the hind's belongings look in that leafy vale in the grey dawn of an autumn morning. To *rim* means to move, to go away, as "I mun rim somewhere just now, I reckon, though I mortal hate rimmin' —it's unked."

As might readily be imagined, having in mind the isolated and lonely character of some portions of Shakespeare's greenwood, that word *unked* is constantly tripping from the rustic's tongue. Speaking of a certain farm one day my shepherd friend said to me, "'Tis a mortal unked place, I can tell thee.

There's 'ardly a cow's head on it, so you can tell."

In Warwickshire the word *unked* is used in a variety of ways. It is applied to person, animal, place, or thing. One meaning of the term is lonely, dull, solitary, as " I feel unked wi' no one to speak to." Another applies to scenes and sights. A maiden will say, " Hey, I had such an unked dream last night " ; in fact, the general signification of the word seems to be that anything of an unpleasing nature is *unked* in the understanding of these picturesque and superstitious woodlanders.

The, what I may call, poetic touch in the language of Shakespeare's greenwood is very happily seen in the word *favours*. No true born peasant of leafy Warwickshire ever neglects the use of this pretty term. When two mothers are discussing the comeliness of a child at the garden gate of the cottage, one of them is sure to say, " I think she favours her feyther." To *favour* is to look like, to resemble. " 'Tis sed I favour you, mother, more nor feyther," a fond daughter will cry with delight (her mother being pretty) ; and in like manner the shepherd, after tracing the lineaments and points of a lamb, will sagely remark, "I judge as her favours her dam."

That word *judge*, too, so extensively used by the peasantry, has quite a Shakespearean ring about it. What, for example, could be prettier than the expression of an aged mother to her family, "God bless all on ye. I judged as ye'd be comin' to see me this motherin'"? In another sense *judge* is used in the form of an accusation, as "I judge ye o' tellin' that lie." To judge literally means to think or to accuse, and the sense in which it is uttered has quite a different charm when issuing from the tongue of the rustic.

Living so far in the core of Nature's heart it may be that the dweller in Shakespeare's greenwood has become what Gilbert White would call a "stationary man"—devoted alike to his language and his soil. Certain it is that the homely speech written more than three centuries ago by the great Stratford-on-Avon dramatist is practically the same as that spoken to-day. And the manners, moreover, are much the same, as I will show by one simple illustration.

Human nature being akin at any time, or

under any condition, it is, perhaps, by no means remarkable that sometimes the Warwickshire lasses will fall out and quarrel with one another. In such a case one of the girls is almost sure to say, "I'll set my ten commandments in your face," which in more plain language means "I'll scratch your face." A saying, this, as old as Shakespeare; for in the Second Part of "King Henry the Sixth" (Act I. scene 3), occurs the following couplet, where the Duchess of Gloster says to Queen Margaret:

Could I come near your beauty with my nails,
I'd set my ten commandments in your face.

Though this manner may not be strictly confined to this greenwood, it is decidedly expressive, if inelegant, and has the warrant of the poet for its continued observance in his native woodland.

As an apt exemplification of the poetry of the so-called "common tongue" of the Warwickshire rustic, the term *deaf-nut* may be cited. The real meaning of the term is a hollow nut—a nut without a kernel; but the dormant poetical instinct implanted in the breast of the Arden peasant gives it a higher significance and applies it to affections of the heart.

When a Warwickshire maiden's young man has left her to seek his fortune at "gay Brookington," or elsewhere, she will say with a demure face, "Hey, my life's that holler now; it's like a deaf-nut from Cuddington 'Ood," dropping the "w" in wood in the manner usual with the natives of this greenwood. A mother's heart is like a *deaf-nut*, void and cold, when her child's love has gone from it. So poetical a dialect phrase as *deaf-nut* has, indeed, quite a Shakespearean ring about it, and might well have come from the tongue and pen of the poet himself.

Singularly expressive, too, is the word *tooting*, so often heard tripping from the tongue of the rustic housewife. "Donna thee come tootin' about arter my lad, Jacobina," a mother will say, "othergates I shall tell thy feyther, an' then ye'll get it mortal ill-convenient, I mek no dout." In the meaning of the Warwickshire rustic to "*toot* about" is to hang, to slink, to sidle, and to idle about; sometimes with a precise object in view (as when Jacobina desires to wheedle Jack into taking her to the Warwickshire Statute Fair—"the Mop," as she would call it), at other times without it.

The range of subjects and objects to which *toot* and *tooting* may be applied is very wide indeed; from the bailiff *tooting* about the farm buildings before taking possession, to the ancient grimalkin who *toots* about the dairy in the hope of surreptitiously enjoying a dish of new cream.

The word *brevet*, though lacking the individuality of *toot*, is often used in exchange with that word and has a somewhat similar significance. "Now donna thee brevet about that rick-straddle, or thee'lt hev it on top o' thee," is a sentence that may be often heard in a Warwickshire harvest field. Literally the word *brevet* is to sniff about like a dog, but common usage has applied the word to any person or creature of an inquisitive nature, and even the parsons of certain villages in Shakespeare's greenwood have been accused of "brevettin' their noses inter the business of other folks."

An illustration of the quaintness and

simplicity of the Warwickshire rustic dialect is happily shown in the expressive, almost pictorial word *othergates*, which is so readily heard issuing from the mouths of Strephon and Phyllis. In the language of these poetic rustics *othergates* is a substitution for otherwise, in another manner. If you cannot do a thing this way you must do it that. If this gate is closed that may be open. "Ye mun do what I tell thee, othergates—" meaning that if you do not, some other way must be found to make you do it. The strength and simplicity of this word is not a little remarkable, and as it is spoken by the rustic, sometimes with a shake of the head to foreshadow the cost of a broken rule, it has that certain picturesque effect so peculiar to the Warwickshire dialect.

Certainly one of the quaintest words in the language of this classic greenwood is the word *colly*. The townsman would surely say that the word stood for a very well-known member of the canine race, which the Warwickshire shepherd invariably has sidling at his heels. If he were wandering down one of these leafy hidden lanes some morning when a dark gloomy sky hung overhead, and were to get into conversation with a chance native, it would not be long ere he would be entirely disillusioned; for the rustic when speaking of the weather (a subject upon which the dweller in Shakespeare's greenwood is always the spokesman and prophet of his own country) he would be almost sure to say, "'Tis a mortal colly mornin', sir, inna it?"

It will thus be seen that when the Warwickshire peasant speaks of "a *colly* mornin'," he means a dark, black morning. Anything gloomy, dull, or oppressive is, to him, a *colly* thing. A dark night is a *colly* night; a black horse, cow, sheep, or dog is a "*colly* 'un," as the case may be; and whenever the prospect of the rustic's life is at all a shadowed one, it is for him a "*colly* outlook." This word is as quaint as it is singular, and shows the dwellers in this delightful greenwood in quite characteristic vein.

As a specimen of the enduring qualities of the Warwickshire rustic dialect, instance may be made of the popularly current word *mortal*. At the Mothering or the Thomasing this word is richly in evidence, and is full of warmth, sympathy, and pathos. "Hey, I'm mortal glad to see thee," will cry the fond mother to her daughter newly arrived from some outlying farmstead, and the daughter will invariably reply, "So are I glad to see thee, mother, though I were mortal afraid as I shouldna be able to come, 'cause o' the floods bein' out."

The *mortal glad* of the rural dweller is the extremely glad of the resident in town. *Mortal*, as the rustic means it, is the extreme in everything. Now this word *mortal*, with precisely the same signification as now attaches to it, was used by Shakespeare in "As You Like It" (Act II. scene 4), where Touchstone says: "We that are true lovers run into strange capers; but as all is mortal in Nature, so is all Nature in love mortal in folly," meaning extreme in folly.

With this fine and expressive example of the enduring power of the language of Shakespeare's greenwood, these selections, giving the principal characteristics of the dialect, must be brought to a close. They are taken at random with a view to making this account interesting as well as informing ; but they will, I think, suffice to evince clearly the grip, the directness, and the picturesque quality of the dialect of this classical county. There are few tongues so exclusive and so little susceptible to change as the tongue of the Warwickshire peasant, and yet, as I have pointed out, this county, called by Drayton, "The Heart of England," is perhaps more assailed by the influence of change than many other shires not so frequently visited by travellers of mixed nationalities.

It was never my intention to make this set of selections a series of stereotyped dictionary words. Rather was it my desire, as previously stated, to make a few bright and apposite jottings upon a subject, which, while deeply interesting, has had far too little attention paid to it ; and my hope is that the wish has been realised. My claims for the dialect of the Warwickshire rustic are that it is a strong, expressive, poetical, picturesque, simple, and enduring language, and more nearly allied to the language of the English Bible and the works of Shakespeare than the dialect of any other English county.

The Superstitions

The Vale of the Red Horse.—The Fateful Magpie.—
The Rollright Stones.—The Last Warwickshire Witch.
—The Famous Witch-Sticking at Long Compton and
Tysoe.—The Ilmington Hills.—The Devil in Ilmington.
—The Poisoning of Sir Thomas Overbury, a Native.—
The Night Coach and Night Hounds.—One-Handed
Boughton.—His Ghost caught in a Phial and "laid" in
a Marl Pit.—Seeing the Phantom Coach-and-Six.—Mr.
Snell's Opinion.—Squire Newsham's Ghost and Night
Coach.—The Superstitions of Guy's Cliffe.—The Ghost
of Piers Gaveston.—The Ghastly Procession to Blacklow
Hill.—The White Woman of Chesford Bridge.—The
Dial House Murder.—The Murder at Littleham Bridge.
—The Hole that cannot be Filled.—Clopton House.—
The Clopton Vault in Stratford-on-Avon Church.—The
Tragic Death of Charlotte Clopton (the Juliet of
Shakespeare).—The Drowning of Margaret Clopton (the
Ophelia of Shakespeare).—The Ghosts' Walk.—The
Murder of a Monk in the Clopton Oratory.—The Spirit
of the Wych Elm.

The Superstitions

IF it is remarkable, and I think it is, that the dialect form of speech now in vogue in rural Warwickshire should have survived for a period of between three and four hundred years, it is also noteworthy that the superstitions should have existed for a like term, and should still survive in some of their most famous forms at the end of the nineteenth century—in an age which plumes itself upon its civilisation and enlightenment. This is the more remarkable bearing in mind the fact that Warwickshire is the central county of England, open to all the influences of modern progress, and, in many seasons of the year, simply overrun with visitors, who might be supposed to bring with them the new ideas, the new fancies, and the new forms of speech of a new people.

The survival of superstition is, I think, to be traced to the original loneliness and woodiness of leafy Warwickshire, which made it a dark land in which nature could display her many moods both night and day ; and these would, no doubt, operate strongly upon the minds of the simple, almost primeval, woodlanders, with an energetic and perhaps a fatal effect ; because people who are cut off, as it were, from all civilising influences are more prone than townspeople to regard the movements of natural life as evidences of the supernatural, and to associate with an invisible and evil agency the simple workings of the laws of Nature.

Yet the curious fact remains that the most famous survivals of superstitions and witchcraft in Warwickshire have occurred in the picturesque Vale of the Red Horse which lies in the Feldon, or "open country," south of the Avon ; whereas the Woodland, which embraces the ancient Forest of Arden, is on the north side of the river, and although superstition in many forms is rife there to-day, the more celebrated cases are indigenous to the soil of the south—growing out of Shakespeare's own immediate neighbourhood, and are, perhaps, to be traced to the close proximity of the Rollright Stones, to and around which so much superstitious glamour continues to cling.

What I may suitably call the gentler forms of superstitious feeling are common to both Woodland and Feldon. The forester, the ploughman, the shepherd, the milk-boy, the field girl, the housewife, and indeed all peasants of whatever age, condition, or calling will turn their money (if they have any, if not they will borrow two halfpence for the occasion) "for luck" at hearing the first note of the cuckoo. The waggoner, returning home to his cottage in a coomb on a summer evening, after a hard day's work, would feel uneasy in mind if *one* magpie instead of *two* flew over his head. He would persuade himself that sorrow was in store for him. In his simple country jargon :

> One magpie means sorrow ;
> Two mirth ;
> Three a wedding ;
> And four a birth.

So when he saw the one magpie, the fateful one, he would cross himself or raise his hat to the bird to prevent the bad luck which otherwise would be sure to follow his neglect.

Such forms of superstition as these, and many others to which I shall subsequently allude in the course of this account, are observed by the peasants in all the villages and hamlets of Warwickshire ; so far, however, as an intimate knowledge of the life of the peasant in this delightful country has enabled me to discover, it is only in the Vale of the Red Horse, and more especially in, and in the immediate vicinity of, the villages of Kineton, Tysoe, and Long Compton, that superstition amounting to an unslayable faith in witchcraft has existed in an acute form through the centuries down to the past twenty years, and still survives, in spite of the march

The Superstitions 65

of education and civilising influences, with a strength that is almost dangerous.

Perhaps the environments of the village of Long Compton have something to do with the survival there to this day of a staunch belief in witchcraft. It is just on the southern border line of leafy Warwickshire, is planted in a gentle hollow, and is quite close to the King Stone of the Rollrights, which have so long fostered superstition in the minds of the lowly peasants. The community, too, is extremely small, and is practically untouched by the enlightening influences of modern education; so that living so out of the world, with the weird and witch-cherishing circle of stones for companions, the peasant's minds become clouded with those "thick-coming fancies" which such a life is likely to beget.*

Less than twenty-five years ago, to be precise in September 1875, there were in the opinion of James Heywood, a native and resident, no less than sixteen witches in the village of Long Compton. The man was not

* Mr. Arthur Evans' paper (*Folk-Lore*, March 1895) gives a full account of the interesting customs and superstitions which centre round the Rollright Stones.

singular in his opinions; many others shared the same extraordinary belief, though they were more passive in their actions than the man Heywood. In the same village there had lived from her birth to the age of eighty years a woman of the peasant class, named Ann Tennant.

Whether the weight of her years and her hard-working life had rendered her as uncomely in person as those two famous Lancashire witches, Mother Demdike and Mother Chattox, whom Harrison Ainsworth has made such weird characters, or whether circumstances had conspired to alienate her from her neighbours are matters about which I need not trouble the reader. Suffice it to say that by some means the poor old lady had drawn upon herself the unwelcome attentions of certain villagers, who, led by the modern Warwickshire witch-hunter, James Heywood, and filled with the superstition of the neighbourhood, became firmly convinced that she had the evil eye and was "a proper witch."

No doubt the man, ignorant boor though he was, had imbibed some knowledge of witches and of the manner of testing them. It is clear, indeed, that he had determined to test, or rather to kill, Dame Tennant; for chancing to meet her out one day gathering sticks for the coming winter, he stabbed her with a pitchfork, saying at the same time that he "would kill all the damned witches in Long Compton, and that there were sixteen on 'em." He did, in sober truth, kill Dame Tennant, witch or no witch, for he stabbed her so severely with the pitchfork that the wound proved fatal, and the poor victim of deeply rooted superstition died almost immediately.

How surely the cloud of superstitious belief had fallen upon the mind of this man was shown in the defence he made for the murder he had committed. "If you know," he said, "the number o' people who lies i' our churchyard, who, if it had not been for them (the witches), would be alive now, you would be surprised. Her (the deceased) was a proper witch." His mind was thickly overlaid with supernaturalism. He saw witches everywhere—in everything. When the water was brought to him in the police cell, he roundly declared there were witches in it.

For years, it was stated, this man had held the belief that horses, cows, sheep, and other cattle sickening and dying, or ill-fortune befalling any of his neighbours, was the result of " the evil eye " of some of the unfortunate old women of the place whom he designated as " proper old witches " ; and it appeared from the evidence that this craze was more or less believed in, according to the degree in which the mind was coloured with superstition, by at least one-third of the inhabitants of the village.

Heywood's method of attacking the supposed witch was probably a reminiscence of the official "pricking" procedure of the seventeenth century witch-finder. In most parts of England where a belief in witchcraft has existed this has been the form which the testing has taken.

The year 1875 was quite a witch year in the Vale of the Red Horse. All the little lonely villages, clustering there in silence and suspicion, were bitten with the craze for witch-finding. Whether Long Compton started the cry or not, cannot well be determined ; but it passed mysteriously from village to village and made a very sad time for ancient dames. There seems to have been no suspicion that any of the old men, or young men of shady character, were warlocks. Only the women were accused of possessing the evil eye.

One such suffered at the village of Tysoe, a short distance from Long Compton. She was, it is stated, reputed by her neighbours to be a witch; so much so that some people came over from Brailes, an adjacent village, and taking her unawares, scored her hand with a corking-pin, in order, as they said, to nullify the effects of the evil eye which she had cast upon them, when they met her out one day.

To draw blood was always the favourite method of dealing with supposed witches. That there were persons thought to possess the power of witchcraft in Warwickshire, and that blood was drawn from them three hundred years ago, may be assumed from the fact that Shakespeare alludes to the practice in the First Part of "King Henry the Sixth," when he makes Talbot say to La Purcell:

*Blood will I draw on thee, thou art a witch,
And straightway give thy soul to him thou serv'st.*

It is an interesting though painful fact, therefore, to notice that blood should have been drawn from a supposed witch in Shakespeare's greenwood so recently as the year 1875.

A neighbourhood so completely under the dominion of a belief in supernatural agencies could not for long exist without imparting a kindred spirit to folk living somewhat farther afield; and so we find that the strange, barren, and old-world village of Ilmington (of which the once celebrated Rev. Julian Young, a relative of the eminent tragedian, Charles Mayne Young, was Vicar), eight miles south-west of Stratford-on-Avon, was in the toils of superstition. Not that the survivals of a faith in witchcraft, manifested so dramatically at Long Compton and Tysoe, were the creation of a similar spirit in the minds of the isolated folk at Ilmington, for superstitious feeling owing to the uncouth environment of the inhabitants had long been known there; but it is possible that the witch-killing and witch-scoring cases of the former villages accentuated the influence in the uncanny which already possessed them, and made them have a still firmer faith in the weird stories of their own village.

As I have said, it is doubtless the environments of the village of Ilmington which fixes gloomy and foreboding fancies in the minds of the peasantry. The parish lies in a coomb at the foot of the Ilmington Hills, a spur of the main chain of the Cotswolds, about which so much so-called supernatural mystery has long hung ; and which not more than a few years ago (if we are to believe the evidence of a family living under the hills) produced a female ghost of exceptional beauty. With the "unked hills," as they are called in the local patois, growing above them in solitary and gloomy grandeur, it is not a matter for wonder that superstition should so haunt the minds of the peasants resident there.

Something of the utterly isolated and solitary character of this neighbourhood may be gathered from an observation made from the pulpit of the ancient parish church there by a London clergyman during the tenure of the Rev. Julian Young in the 'fifties and 'sixties. The Vicar was absent from home, and the minister who was doing duty for him, struck by the remoteness and seclusion of the parish, said in one of his sermons :

"That on looking down upon the village from a neighbouring height, he thought that surely the Devil could never have found his way over the hills to that peaceful, out-of-the-world hamlet, but found on investigation that he had been forestalled, and that his old foe had been for some time in possession and was quite at home there."

The divine was not far wrong. The devil of superstition had long had a firm hold upon the minds of the peasants of this neighbourhood, in the midst of which was born the celebrated author and contemporary of Shakespeare, Sir Thomas Overbury, whose death by poison, in 1613, in the Tower of London, was encompassed through the influence of the Earl of Rochester and the Countess of Essex ; all the strange stories of the hills which had been current for generations, and are still heard in the mouths of the aged, were implicitly believed in ; and there were those to be found who would swear to having seen the preternatural sights, such as the more enlightened mind is fain to look upon as the workings of an over-lively and disordered imagination ; and as it was then, so it is almost the same now, in the dark, little, hilled-in hamlet of Ilmington.

Superstition in Warwickshire has from a very early period associated itself with a staunch belief in the appearance of the " Night Coach." This is a form of vision-seeing common in woody districts, and similar to the spectral apparition of " the boggart" which was formerly asserted to have been so often seen in the neighbourhood of Meridan—anciently called " the Miry Den " because of its swampy condition—which is seated in the thick portion of the once famous Forest of Arden.

A " Night Coach " is recorded to have nightly driven over the flats and hills in the district of the villages of Mickleton, on the Gloucestershire border, and Ilmington within the boundary line of leafy Warwickshire. Many people staunchly averred that they saw this phantom coach, and even to this day the memory of it remains deeply rooted in the minds of the old and solitary inhabitants ; the uncanny story having been told to them by their superstition-enthralled ancestors.

This coach has been described, by those who professed to have seen it, as a heavy family coach, at that date (somewhere about 1870) grown old-fashioned, and drawn by six horses. Its course was over the springy turf of the hills towards the Gloucestershire boundary of the county ; whence it passed abruptly over the brow of the steep hills into the depths below, in a manner which never could have been performed by an earthly coach, drawn by six natural horses and driven by a natural coachman.

Though the performances of this night coach (which was said to be sometimes followed by a spectral pack of "Night Hounds") took place upon the extreme edge of the south-eastern boundary of Warwickshire, the effect of them upon the villagers living along the Vale of the Red Horse in their woody, low-pitched, and out-of-the-world position, could only be to heighten and accentuate the superstitious feeling under which they already existed.

Indeed, I am sometimes disposed to think that there may be traced some connection between this "Night Coach" and the famous spectral six-in-hand of the equally famous Elizabethan knight, One-handed Boughton, of Lawford Hall, near Rugby, in the northwest district of Warwickshire, as this coach appeared about the same date and made its excursions during the nocturnal hours, which was, of course, quite natural in regard to a phantom coach.

What the particular cause of the nightly racings of One-handed Boughton was, cannot be precisely determined; but that his spirit was by some means violently exercised, and that men of light and leading firmly believed in the apparition, may be assumed from the fact that several Warwickshire gentlemen and clergymen met together one night when One-handed Boughton was taking his nightly ride, and by bell, and book, and prayer, succeeded in catching his perturbed spirit, and enclosed it in a phial which they threw into a neighbouring marl-pit filled with water.

It is said that the father of Sir Theodosius

Boughton (the young man who, in 1780, was poisoned with laurel-water by his brother-in-law, Captain Donnellan) had so much faith in the truth of this legend, that when a neighbour of his, Sir Francis Skipworth, applied to him for permission to drain the pit with the object of seeing whether there were any fish therein—he being a devoted follower of Isaac Walton—the Baronet emphatically refused, saying that "his ancestor, One-handed Boughton rested there and should not be disturbed." The pond, however, was subsequently drained, the phial containing the spirit of the old possessor of the Hall was recovered, and was stated to have been given into the keeping of a descendant of his—Mr. Boughton Leigh of Brownsover Hall, an adjacent edifice.

As showing the grip which these old-time superstitions have upon the mind of the Warwickshire rustic (though it must be admitted that there is something mysterious and unexplainable in this case of One-handed Boughton, which reminds one of the speech which Shakespeare puts into the mouth of Hamlet, "There are more things in heaven and earth, Horatio, than are dreamt of in your philosophy ") it may be of interest to note that in the early 'seventies, though the old Hall at Lawford had long since been razed to the ground, there was a revival of the belief in the ghostly visitation of One-handed Boughton, and it exists to this day in the vicinity of Rugby.

There is a report current that an old gentleman named Wolfe, living in, or near, Long Lawford (who died in 1871, at the age of nearly a hundred years) well remembered that one day when sitting by his mother's side at King's Newnham, a village hard by, a man rushed into the cottage out of breath and exclaimed, "I've just seen One-handed Boughton. I saw him coming and opened the gate for him, but he flew over in a carriage of six." The man was perfectly convinced of the truth of the vision he had seen, and nothing could persuade him that he had not beheld the redoubtable One-handed Boughton, who had resided at Lawford Hall in the days of Good Queen Bess, and appears to haunt the scene of his former abode to this day.

Another instance was afforded by a Mr. John Watts, an old and respected inhabitant of Rugby, who died about the year 1863, aged ninety-three. He was, it is said, one day out walking with a friend in the neighbourhood honoured by the appearance of One-handed Boughton, when the friend suddenly started, and pointing to a distance cried, "There is One-handed Boughton!" Mr. Watts averred that he stared with all his might in the direction indicated, but *he* could see nothing whatever.

This example of one man seeing what another could not, reminds me of the humorous description of the mystery of seeing and not seeing ghosts, which George Eliot has introduced in her Warwickshire novel "Silas Marner," and which bears upon the subject of superstitions in Shakespeare's greenwood. The scene is laid in the bar parlour of "The Rainbow" at Raveloe, where the conversation on the spectral performances known as "Cliffe's Holiday," has so excited the guests that Mr. Snell, the landlord, deems it prudent to pour oil upon the troubled waters by means of the following sage remarks :

"There's folks i' my opinion, they can't see ghos'es—not if they stood as plain as a pikestaff before 'em. And there's reason i' that. For there's my wife now, can't smell, not if she'd the strongest o' cheese under her nose. I never seed a ghost myself: but then I says to myself, 'Very like I haven't got the smell for 'em.' I mean puttin' a ghost for a smell or else contrariways. And so I'm for holding with both sides; for as I say, the truth lies between 'em. And if Dowlas was to go and stand and say he'd never seed a wink o' Cliff's Holiday all the night through, I'd back him; and if anybody said as Cliff's Holiday was certain sure for all that, I'd back him too. For the smell's what I go by."

There were evidently many persons in the neighbourhood of Lawford Hall who had what Mr. Snell called "a smell" for ghosts. They not only smelt out and saw the ghost of One-handed Boughton, but when, after the murder of Sir Theodosius, the possessors decided to demolish the Hall as a thing accursed, the belief in the presence of the spectre was so strong in the minds of the inhabitants that it was with the greatest difficulty that workmen could be obtained to pull down the edifice.

The Vale of the Red Horse had also its "Night Coach," which was no more than natural in a locality so rife with feelings of superstition; and this, perhaps, is the most interesting of those which are said to have been seen in Warwickshire, because it dates from quite modern times and is even now believed in by the dwellers in the scenes of its nocturnal visits.

At one and a half miles from the village of Kineton, having in front of it an ornamental piece of water with a picturesque island in the middle, stands the ancient edifice known as Chadshunt House, the ancestral seat of the Newsham family. From what can be gathered the old Squire, who died so late ago as 1836, seems to have been a noted character in the neighbourhood, given somewhat to the then current tastes for sport and the cup. Soon after his death the story went abroad that a ghostly coach and four (not the spectral six horses this time) with Squire Newsham holding "the ribbons" was seen or heard to ride down the avenue in the Park and then suddenly vanished from the sight and completely died out of the hearing.

What the Chadshunt Squire had done in his lifetime to be so restless after death is not easily to be determined, but it is certain that within the last seventeen years, explain it as you may, several educated persons testify to having distinctly heard sounds resembling those of invisible horses and of an invisible vehicle turning on the site of the old gravel sweep.

Though to the city dweller who rarely, if ever, finds himself in the dark, these weird stories of spectral coaches and horses racing like mad in the dead watches of the night, may seem fanciful, if not absurd, the effect is amazingly different to those who live in what may be called the solitary nooks of Nature, where gaslights have not yet come, and where everything, even to the shape of the trees, contributes to the feeling of awe already existent in the peasant's mind; and in many parts of woody Warwickshire the phenomena appearing at intervals are so strange, and, as it seems, inexplicable, that the growth and continuance of what is not infrequently the grossest superstition in the minds of these country dwellers, is rather a subject for pity than for surprise.

It is probably the still leafy and undulating condition of Warwickshire that has caused so many of the current superstitions to become connected with out-of-door life. There are strange beliefs in haunted houses, and it would be strange if there were not, in a county so rich in historic mansions, each of which has its own particular romance, and many of which have their own familiar spirit.

But where the superstitious hold upon the peasant mind is greater is in the vicinity of ancient fabrics whose character is shadowed by the gloom of some grim story that has come down through the ages; by isolated copse, wood, or bridge; or in remote lanes fringed with tall elms and overgrown with tangle, where some dark deed of bloodshed, committed in the past, has woven a cloud of superstition and fear which generally results in the so-called "appearance" of a ghostly visitant to some of the rustics. And whether this spectre of the spirit-world is really seen or is merely the figment of a weak and susceptible imagination does not in the least matter. It is enough that such a thing has been even suggested to make the rustic's belief in it as strong as his belief in the proof of Holy Writ.

Thus we find, and not unnaturally when the romance and history of the place is recalled, that the spirit-glamour has settled down upon the ancient seat known as Guy's Cliffe (one mile from Warwick by the Coventry Road), now the residence of Lord Algernon Percy, brother of the Duke of Northumberland; and also over Blacklow Hill, a slight eminence a little distance northwest of the Cliffe House.

This very picturesque edifice, charmingly seen at the end of a venerable avenue of Scotch firs, is, as every reader of English and Warwickshire history is probably aware, the scene in which is laid the romantic story of Guy, Earl of Warwick, whose exploits in love and war form a subject, which, if mythical, as antiquarians declare, has nevertheless developed into a belief which centuries have not removed, and which no amount of antiquarian discussion can exorcise; and Blacklow Hill is the historic spot in which the witty, light-hearted, and unscrupulous Gaul, Piers Gaveston, Earl of Cornwall and favourite of Edward the Second, lost his head at the instigation of Guy de Beauchamp, Earl of Warwick (called by Gaveston "the Black Dog of Arden"), and other powerful barons; so that the survival of superstitions in and around this spot, is, as I have said, not unnatural.

Hard by Blacklow Hill there is a tract of waste land called Ganerslie Heath. No peasant will linger there after nightfall, for strange sounds are said to be heard issuing through the thick foliage, sounds which fill the rustic mind with fearful bodings. At the dread hour of midnight, it is averred that dismal bells toll from Blacklow Hill, and as the palfrey upon which Gaveston was led to execution there was richly caparisoned and wore a string of bells round its neck, superstition has come to regard this sound as proceeding from the spectre of man and horse, which during the past five hundred years is supposed to have traversed the road from Warwick Castle to the place of execution—

just as the gruesome cavalcade did in real life upon that doomed midnight or early morning.

In confirmation of the phantom sights said to have been seen, and still believed in, in the neighbourhood of Guy's Cliffe and Blacklow Hill, a formerly well-known resident of Warwick, whose relatives occupied official positions there and who, in 1892, was living at Horsham and Ringmere in Sussex, has sent me the following notes :

"The neighbourhood of Guy's Cliffe in my young days bore a somewhat uncanny repute. As children we hastened from it at dusk of evening, perhaps a little with the qualified feeling of Madame de Staël when she said of ghosts, ' Je n'y crois pas, mais je les crains.' There were different versions of what 'appeared' in this neighbourhood. One story narrated that a lady was seen at night to pass from the little gate on the right of the avenue, to cross the road and vanish in the opposite gardens. Another version told of a band of armed men being seen on the road and disappearing on the ascent to the hill.

"One assertive witness, an aged woman of spectral aspect, was well known to me in early boyhood, and by her it was related with unfailing credence. She was the wife of a soldier, and when she, with others, witnessed the phenomenon, she was walking out with them to meet the returning lovers and husbands whose arrival was expected by Coventry, and she, as I personally know, unwaveringly believed in the apparition spectacle which then appeared. Mr. Frederick Enoch, a native of Warwick, has versified this tradition as follows :

> "*Suddenly through the midnight haze,*
> *Up along the Guy's Cliffe way,*
> *Passed before the women's gaze*
> *Horsemen, in a weird array.*
>
> "*Not a sound could any hear,*
> *While the cortege glided past;*
> *And the women—smote with fear—*
> *Gazed in silence as it passed.*
>
> "*As it passed, as leading there*
> *He—a minion, fortune's fool—*
> *In the hour of last despair,*
> *Scorned—an object of misrule.*

> "*So it passed, till lost again,*
> *Fading in the mead so still,*
> *Where Piers Gaveston was slain*
> *On the mount of Blacklow Hill.*"

North of this historic, and (in the night) uncouth hill, on the road leading from Leamington to Kenilworth, there is a bridge over the river known as Chesford Bridge, originally built in the thirteenth century by the Abbots of Coomb Abbey. Clumps of woodland of a rather tangled and uncanny aspect flank the western side of the bridge, and, as might be expected of such a spot, it has long had its familiar spirit.

The figure of a woman (ghosts, I have found, are in Warwickshire more often of the gentler than the sterner sex) is stated to have been seen crossing the road from the Dial House Farm, on the right of the highway to the dark woodlet on the left, where it immediately vanished. Dwellers in the scattered cottages of the neighbourhood fight shy of Chesford Bridge after dark, and although many of them have doubtless never seen the apparition which is said to "walk," the story has obtained such possession of their minds that they hold an unslayable belief in it.

As one who has delved much into the bygone history of Warwickshire, I may here mention that in the year 1820, a very sensational tragedy took place at the Dial House Farm; a woman named Ann Hawtrey, employed probably as a domestic there, having in a barbarous manner taken the life of her mistress, Mrs. Dormer, whose descendants still occupy the house. The unhappy murderess is described as being the possessor of some personal beauty, but this did not save her from the gallows (as no doubt it helped to save Hetty Sorrel, who was sentenced to death in St. Mary's Hall, Coventry, though never executed, as readers of "Adam Bede" are aware), for she was hanged at Warwick on April 20 of that year, in the presence of ten thousand people.

Probably the appearance of the "White Lady" of Chesford Bridge may be traced to the above gruesome fact, for it is notorious that scenes of deeds of bloodshed in the minds of the peasants living in or near the spot invariably become haunted, either by the spirit of the murderer or by that of the murdered person, and in this case it may be that the spirit of the miserable woman, in remorse for her crime, visits the scenes of her former abode, and in the glimpses of the moon moans and sighs round the house and then disappears in the darkness of the adjacent thicket.

A curious superstition which amounts to the firmest belief surrounds a structure called "Littleham Bridge," a lonely spot on the high road between Stratford-on-Avon and Hampton Lucy. Here on the night of November 4, 1820, Mr. William Hirons, a yeoman of the neighbouring village of Alveston, was set upon and murdered by four ruffians. He was found dead in the morning with his head resting in a hole; and from that day to this, a period of seventy-five years, every attempt to fill the hole again has, it is said, been ineffectual.

This is the local belief and affirmation. If the hole is filled with earth at night it is empty again the next morning. What strange being or power performs this nocturnal act, no man knoweth; but that it is the foundation of a very deeply rooted superstition can be ascertained by any one who visits the spot and inquires about the tragedy and the hole from the inhabitants of the locality. The four men were arrested, tried, found guilty, and hanged at Warwick in April 1821; and a fact as weird as the existence of the hole is that one of the murderers was Thomas Hawtrey, the brother of Ann Hawtrey, who was executed almost exactly a year previously, for the murder of Mrs. Dormer of the Dial House Farm, Chesford Bridge.

Superstitions in regard to haunted houses in Warwickshire are too numerous to be dealt with in anything like detail. As being more closely associated with Shakespeare's greenwood, however, and as the circumstances were more than probably known to the poet himself, the stories connected with Clopton House, near Stratford-on-Avon (the present seat of Sir Arthur Hodgson, K.C.M.G.), may here be opportunely alluded to.

Clopton House, about a mile and a half north-west of Shakespeare's birthplace, was formerly the Manor House of the ancient Clopton family, who obtained a grant of the property in the thirteenth century. The present house dates from the time of Henry the Seventh ; the only portion of this date, however, that now remains, is a porchway entrance, through which it is almost certain that Shakespeare and his companions must often have passed.

The two stories connected with the Ladies Charlotte and Margaret Clopton (both of which must have been known to Shakespeare, the first of which he is thought to have utilised in " Romeo and Juliet," and the other in " Hamlet ") are of a character so romantic and lamentable that it is no wonder they should have added the phantom touch to the old edifice. Both ladies, indeed, have enjoyed the reputation of having " walked " in spirit about the house and grounds of their home ever since their untimely deaths more than three hundred years ago.

The scene of Charlotte Clopton's tragic story is laid at Stratford-on-Avon during the Black Plague which greatly decimated the population of the classic town in 1564, and which, no doubt, was the means of many persons being buried alive in Warwickshire.

In his "Visits to Remarkable Mansions," William Howitt alludes to the story in the following words:

"In the time of some epidemic, the sweating sickness or the plague (the Black Plague), this young girl sickened, and, to all appearance, died. She was buried with fearful haste in the vault of Clopton Chapel, attached to Stratford Church; but the sickness was not stayed. In a few days another of the Cloptons died, and him too they bore to the ancestral vault; but as they descended the gloomy stairs, they saw by the torchlight, Charlotte Clopton in her grave clothes leaning against the wall. And when they looked nearer she was indeed dead; but not before, in the agonies of despair and hunger, she had bitten a piece of flesh from her white round arm. Of course she has 'walked' ever since."

Perhaps in all the traditions, superstitions, and legends of the Warwickshire greenwood, there is not one more fearsome and touching than this one, recounting the melancholy fate of beautiful Charlotte Clopton, whose story is said to have been made use of by

Shakespeare in the vault scene of "Romeo and Juliet," though of course he has added the glamour of romance to the picture and laid the scene in Mantua.

If in the case of Charlotte Clopton there are mythical elements which throw doubt on the actuality thereof, it is not so with regard to the mournful fate of Margaret Clopton, whose story Shakespeare has made use of in "Hamlet"; the fair Margaret being thought to be the prototype of the gentle Ophelia. This young and beautiful lady having fallen in love with a man of whom her parent, Sir William Clopton, disapproved, and being forbidden the society of her lover, sought the only method of escape which seems open to love-sick maidens.

"Too much of water hast thou, poor Ophelia," said Laertes, and the same might be said of Margaret Clopton; for being wrought up to agony point, she drowned herself in a pond in the grounds of Clopton House, which is shown you to-day; and the legend runs that the fair young lady's spirit still haunts the scene in the silent watches of the night.

The bluff and jovial Sir Arthur Hodgson, the owner of Clopton, is no believer in the superstition that his hoary mansion is haunted by any spirits but those bright and tangible ones of himself and family. Yet there is one thing in Clopton House to which even he will subscribe his adherence—to wit, that there is something strange and peculiar in regard to that room at the top of the house used as an oratory in the days when the Cloptons were Roman Catholics.

In the remote past, it is said, that a monk was murdered near the top of the staircase, and that his body was dragged along the corridor to be hidden away. A thin dark stain, thought to be the blood of this unfortunate creature, runs from the door of the bedroom to the stairhead, and this is so deeply imprinted in the wood that all attempts to obliterate it have been in vain. That at least is the legend.

With such a grim token of the age of deeds of bloodshed, it is no wonder that the room is looked upon as possessing a spirit-tenant. In 1887 this room (this old-time oratory) was used as a bedroom; but one of

Sir Arthur Hodgson's guests, who undertook to sleep in it, was afterwards heard to declare that he wished never again to experience the grim hospitality of that chamber, because the sounds that he heard throughout the night were of the most terrifying description. Clopton House, therefore, may fairly claim the dignity of possessing a haunted room and the sweet spirits of two beauties of the Elizabethan period.

The gentler superstitions of rural Warwickshire, as I called them at the beginning of this account, are many and various, and deal perhaps more with outdoor than indoor life, though the preternaturalism of cottage life is very strongly marked. That old superstition connected with the wych elm (of which there are so many in Shakespeare's greenwood) seems to be as firmly planted as ever.

There is a story current of a gentleman who went to reside in a remote part of the country. Having cut down a wych elm he told some of his workmen that they could have the branches for firewood. In the course of a week or two he noticed that none of the wood had been removed, and asked the reason. "Why, mister," was the reply, "we donna want the old 'ooman amongst us to be sure." Upon questioning them it appeared that it was a general belief that to burn wych elm would bring down the malignant powers of a witch upon the household.

This reminds me that during a storm some few years ago some boughs were torn from a beautiful wych elm in Offchurch Park, near Leamington, the seat of the Dowager Countess of Aylesford, and they were left for weeks where they fell; none of the peasants living near evincing any desire to remove them to their homes to be used for firewood.

Superstitions regarding birds are very extensive in Warwickshire and very steadfastly entertained. The cuckoo during the winter is changed by rustic faith into the sparrow-hawk; the yellow-hammer is supposed to drink three drops of the devil's blood each May morning; and the robin is believed to have scorched its breast with hell fire, near which it had ventured for a beakful of water to assuage the sufferings of our Saviour when on the Cross.

With this, the prettiest and tenderest of all

the superstitions at present in vogue in leafy Warwickshire, I bring this account to a conclusion. The subject is one that is surrounded with the deepest interest, inasmuch as the bent of rustic feeling in this delightful county towards a belief in the supernatural is, as I have attempted to show, almost as strongly marked to-day, in spite of the wide-reaching influences of civilisation and education, as it was in the days of Shakespeare; though in his time the aspect of rural Warwickshire was more calculated to inspire the mind with eerie feelings than it is now—being wilder, more desolate, and containing fewer dwellers.

The Customs

Street Football at "Milby" on Shrove Tuesday.—The Mothering.—The Mothering Dishes: Stuffed Chine of Pork and Fig Pudding.—The Easter Lifting.—The Lifting and Kissing of Dr. Samuel Parr, LL.D.—The Maying.—The Maying Songs.—The Shakespeare Maypole at Welford.—Sea-Gulls and Schoolboys of Oakfield.—The Beating of the Bounds.—Drum-Beating at Arbury Hall ("The Cheverel Manor" of George Eliot).—Funeral Custom.—Decking Graves with Flowers.—A Sprig of Rosemary.—The Duologues of the Peasantry.—The Harvest Homes.—A Costume Procession.—The Candle-light Auction for Grazing Rights.—The Payment of Wroth Silver at Knightlow Cross.—The Stuffed Marrow for Christmas.—The Roasted Crabs.—The Thomasing.—Humphrey How, the good Porter of Stoneleigh Abbey.—Christmas Carols.—The Mumming.—The Yule Log.—Elder Wine and Hot Toast for Breakfast on Christmas Morning.—Carols for the New Year.—Robert Dover (Director of the Games on Cotswold Hills), a Native of Shakespeare's Greenwood.

The Customs

THOUGH the influence of modern civilisation has, in some instances, made itself felt and has had a depreciating effect upon the customs of the country in certain places, the sequestered position of Shakespeare's greenwood has, in a great measure, rendered it impervious to the revolutions of change ; and in some of the out-of-the-way, hidden villages here may still be seen the quaint and often picturesque customs in which the rude forefathers of the hamlets were wont to take interest and delight.

And not only in the greenwood of Warwickshire are customs practised to-day which date so far back as to render their origin obscure, but in centres of the county which are now busy with the hum and bustle of industry and are the gathering-places of toiling thousands, customs of quaintness and antiquity are still prosecuted, in spite of attempts to put them down, with a vigour which shows no sign of abating.

One of these village customs (now observed in a thriving and thickly-populated town in the hardy North, a town which was once a secluded village and inhabited only by an order of devote nuns) is that of the Shrove Tuesday festival of football, which is played annually in the streets of Nuneaton—the " Milby " of George Eliot's " Scenes of Clerical Life." On the morning of the day the town presents quite a holiday appearance. The shops are shuttered and the young men turn out in hundreds to play their balls through the streets from one end of the town to the other, and win cheers and bright smiles from the faces of their bonnie lassies (the glove-factory girls) who line the pathways in gay attire and kerchief-covered heads.

In the observance of this custom Warwickshire enjoys an almost unique position, since there seems to be only three other places in England (the towns of Dorking in Surrey, and Sedgefield and Chester-le-Street in Durham County) where the practice is carried out. What pancakes have in common with the game of football is a subject as obscure as it is interesting; but it is nevertheless a fact that for an unknown number of years the game of street football has been played in the thoroughfares of this in-Arden town upon the morning of Shrove Tuesday in each year, and at the present time its popularity (in spite of legal measures to suppress it) is as high as it has ever been.

The Shrove Tuesday festival is the first custom of the year in Shakespeare's greenwood. In the proper order of dates (which is the order to be observed in this sketch) the next custom is that of the Mothering. There is, perhaps, in the whole range of customs practised in leafy Warwickshire, nothing quite so touching and sympathetic as this. It is the tie which binds the hearts of the family together—making every member of it one; in feelings, aspirations, thoughts, and sympathies akin; and bringing them all together at least once a year, after the manner of the rhyme used for the occasion.

> *The lad and lass on Mothering Day,*
>   *Hie home to their mother so dear;*
> *'Tis a kiss for she and a kiss for they,*
> *A chine of pork and a sprig of bay,*
>   *A song and dance—but never a tear.*

Exigences of modern life, when some of the young men of the family may be separated from their mothers by hundreds of miles, sometimes make it difficult for the custom of the Mothering to be carried out in the complete manner wished for by the occupants of the picturesque cottage in village or hamlet; but where a few miles only divide the members, the joining of the branches of the family is rigidly adhered to, and the return of the young men and maidens to their parental homes (to the roof-trees beneath which many of them were born) is certainly, from its homely and domestic character, one of the prettiest customs of this poetic greenwood,

The favourite joint for the Mothering is a chine of pork, with stuffing flavoured with a few leaves of the aromatic bay ; and in many cottages this dish is followed by the famous fig pudding, mentioned by Shakespeare. In many an isolated homestead, far in the sequestered solitudes of this evergreen woodland, the preparing of this ancient dish for the table and the palates of the children returning home once again, is a labour of love and great ceremony to the homely cottage woman. Both married and single children observe the custom of the Mothering, and the fourth Sunday in Lent is, indeed, a day of rejoicing under many a thatched roof in leafy Warwickshire.

No more picturesque or mirth-moving custom could well be imagined than the Easter-tide practice of "lifting" which used to be largely in vogue on the village greens of this woodland, and was until recently (and may be so even yet) still extant in some of the more sequestered places where Nature is the only observer of the doings of her children. It may be that the so-called refining influences of modern civilisation have been the means of causing this purely Arcadian custom to fall somewhat into neglect. In any case, what was an annual event, looked forward to with pleasure at the beginning of the century, is, at the end of it, a custom more honoured in the breach than in the observance; a picturesque and merry scene being thus lost to English country life in the most classical of all greenwoods.

The custom in the villages and hamlets of Warwickshire was to hold two liftings—one on Easter Monday, and the other on the following day. On the first day of the junketing the rustic youths "lifted" the lasses—that is, took them up lengthwise in their arms, as a mother would her baby, and kissed them. All were served alike—the buxom, the slender, the comely, the plain, the saucy, and the shy—so that there should be no complaining of more favour being shown to one than to another.

On the second day the girls returned the compliment, and lifted and kissed the young men. There seems to have been even more merriment at the second performance than at the first, inasmuch as some of the young men affected shyness, and so made the fun all the greater.

There is a tradition that early in the present century, when the famous Dr. Samuel Parr was in charge of the cure of Hatton, a village four miles west of Warwick, the young lasses of the neighbourhood were desirous of lifting the classic scholar after the manner of the custom, and that he, affecting the shyness which produced sport, led them a pretty dance over hill and down dale, until they ultimately caught him, lifted him, and exacted the kiss which the practice of the country prescribed. In this the lasses were only observing the strict letter of the law of the custom, for the merry divine had lifted and kissed many of them on the previous day, and it was their turn now to retaliate.

Certainly one of the prettiest customs still in active practice in the shady lanes and on the village greens of leafy Warwickshire is the Maying custom. The method is probably the same in all the counties of rural England in which the Maying is still observed; the only difference may be in the wording of the carols recited upon the occasion.

In Shakespeare's greenwood the general rule is to hold the festival on the twelfth of the month—old May Day. The earlier hours of the previous day are occupied by the children in a perambulation of the parish, calling upon the farm folk and other residents for gifts of flowers and finery with which to decorate their maypoles. In the evening the maypole is hoisted on the village green, or in some paddock or orchard lent for the purpose, and the election of the Queen takes place. Some villages have a King and Queen, but the majority elect a Queen only, thus paying a graceful little compliment to the Royal Lady who sways the sceptre and the hearts of the people of "Merrie England."

On the morrow the Queen and her attendants, as richly bedizened as flowers, ground ivy, May blossoms, and patchwork can make them, again parade the boundary of the parish, singing their May songs (first at the doors of the Squire and Parson, and then at the houses of the lesser people) round a portable maypole ; finally returning to their ground or play-mead, where the songs are sung over again in the following words, to a generally recognised home-made tune.

> 'Tis always on the twelfth of May,
> We meet and dress so gaily;
>   For to-night will merrie be,
>   For to-night will merrie be,
>   For to-night will merrie be,
> We'll sing and dance so gaily.
>
> The sun is up and the morn is bright,
> And the twelfth of May is our delight,
> Then arouse thee, arouse, in the merrie sweet light,
> Take the pail and the labour away.
>
>   That dear little girl,
>   Who lives in yon sky,
>   With the lilies and the roses,
>   Shall never be forgot.
>
> Yonder stands a lovely lady,
> Who she is we do not know,
> Who she is we do not know;
> We will take her for our beauty
> Whether she answers Yes or No.
>
> Then shake the money-box about
> And call on every lady.
>   For to-night will merrie be,
>   For to-night will merrie be,
>   For to-night will merrie be,
> We'll sing and dance so gaily.

After the songs are sung and the day portion of the festival is over, dancing begins, and in some villages (notably in Charlecote, Bidford, Temple Grafton, Hillborough, Long Compton, and other places in the immediate vicinity of Shakespeare's birthplace) the custom is concluded in the Rectory, where children of a larger growth keep up the dance with unflagging energy until the small hours of the next morning in honour of the Queen of the May.

The custom of the Maying wears the dignity of years in Shakespeare's greenwood. In the little border village of Welford (just below the "Hungry Grafton," and adjoining the "Drunken Bidford" of the well-known verse attributed to the poet) there stands, in the centre of a raised mound, encircled by a hedge, a maypole which is regarded as the successor to one around which Shakespeare himself must have danced with his Shottery lass. The existing maypole stands seventy-five feet in height and bears upon the shaft the now faded colours of the red, white and blue "ribbons" which it was the custom to paint upon the pole in the poet's days.

That Shakespeare was fully cognisant of the Maying custom and the practice of painting the maypole seems abundantly clear from the allusion he makes to it in " A Midsummer Night's Dream" (Act III. scene 2) where Hermia thus addresses Helena :

> *And are you grown so high in his esteem,*
> *Because I am so dwarfish, and so low ?*
> *How low am I, thou painted Maypole ?*

As showing how closely feathered life is connected with human life in leafy Warwickshire that curious holiday custom given to the schoolboys of Oakfield, Rugby, may be mentioned at this point ; because in the case referred to the custom was observed in the "merrie month of May," soon after the recurrence of the Maying festival ; and it is my intention to chronicle the events as far as possible in their correct order of date.

Being so far inland it is naturally a rare sight to see a flock of sea-gulls flying over Shakespeare's greenwood, and accordingly whenever a flight of these marine birds (two, three, four, five, or more) is observed the schoolboys of Oakfield can claim a half-holiday. The custom (which was last observed on May 24, 1895, when five sea-gulls were seen flying over the academic shades of Rugby) cannot be traced to its date or organiser, but it is of some antiquity and was evidently instituted by an enthusiastic ornithologist, who wished to inculcate in the minds of the boys of that neighbourhood an abiding love for the birds of the sea and land. A constant look-out is accordingly kept at Oakfield for the passing of the sea-gulls over this inland scene, which is almost as far as it is possible to get from the sea in all England.

An important and often highly humorous and picturesque custom of welcome recurrence in the several parishes of Shakespeare's greenwood is that known as " beating the bounds." In the matter of years this is one of the oldest of country customs, being, in fact, an importation of the Romans, who observed the festival with much ceremony and many religious rites. The season for the observance of this parochial custom in leafy Warwickshire is during Whitsun week; and although formerly, when disputes concerning boundaries of estates and parishes were more rife than they are at the present time, the custom was observed annually, an interval of years is now allowed to pass between one celebration and another, so that the novelty of the event is not staled.

Parson, squire, justice of the peace, parish clerk, village constable, churchwardens, a procession of school children in holiday attire decked with ribbon and flowers, and an individual with a paint-pot and brush; these are the chief actors in the performance of beating the bounds. It is the duty of the latter to mark in flaming red paint the sign of the broad arrow upon the tree-trunk or gate-post which stands upon the boundary line between the two parishes, so that a true record of the extent of the parish may be kept and each may know the particular bush, tree, hurdle, or piece of turf to which it can legally lay claim.

The perambulation of the bounds is sometimes attended with an amount of excitement and humour which is lacking in many other country customs. Brooks have to be forded as best they may be; thatched roofs have to be climbed, walls have to be scaled, and houses have to be passed through —often at inconvenient times; all of which is extremely mirth-provoking to those engaged in honouring the practice. The children, too, have reason to welcome the day of beating the bounds, for at the close of the ceremony it is the rule for the parson or squire of the village to give the small rustics (who with their elders have borne the heat and burden of the day, and with their little figures have marked the boundary line in spots inaccessible to those of larger growth) a feast of nuts and apples, and tea and buns.

Ancestral mansions in Shakespeare's greenwood sometimes have customs of their own. One of these is observed at Arbury Hall, near Nuneaton (the "Cheverel Manor" of George Eliot and the home of the Newdigates), where the beating of a drum to summon the inmates to the table has been customary for a long period. It is suggested that this custom was imported to Arbury in the latter half of the seventeenth century from Blithfield Hall, Rugeley, Staffordshire, by Mary, daughter of Sir Edward Bagot, and first wife of the second Sir Richard Newdigate.

The Customs 115

Whether this is so or not, the custom is a curious one, and deserves a place among the observances which are peculiar to the out-of-the way districts of leafy Warwickshire; where the ancient custom of ringing the curfew at eight o'clock every evening is practised with unfailing regularity, and without which many of the rustics would not know the time for bed—for as Shakespeare says (in "As You Like It") "there is no clock in the forest."

As there are customs that make for joy in life in active use in the greenwood of this leafy county (such as those already described), so there are customs of a pathetic and sympathetic character observed at the close of a life.

For example, there is a well-established practice among the peasant folk of leafy Warwickshire of attending the parish church on the Sunday morning following the death of a relative, the female mourners remaining seated and deeply veiled during the singing of the hymns. This emulation of the custom observed at the singing of the *Dies Iræ*, is so strictly conformed to upon frequent occasions that visitors to the picturesque in-Arden churches here may know at once when a villager has gone to his or her rest, by the number of women seen sitting while the hymns are being sung.

There is a pretty and familiar custom, too, long observed among the villagers of Shakespeare's greenwood, of decking with flowers the graves of dead relatives or friends upon the anniversaries of their birth and death days. The simplicity of this custom is its most charming feature; and certainly there are few more touching sights in the Warwickshire woodland than that of rustic children trooping with pensive steps to the village graveyard to lay their tribute of flowers and rosemary upon the graves of those they loved and have lost.

Among dwellers in this poetic neighbourhood the custom of using sprigs of rosemary both at weddings and burials is still observed, much in the same way as mentioned by Shakespeare in " Romeo and Juliet." Rosemary, indeed, is "for remembrance" in many ways among the Warwickshire peasants. A maiden will give her lover a sprig when the time comes for them to part, and she will receive one from him. The shrub is largely grown in the cottage gardens, and from Shakespeare's days down to the present time it has played an important part in the floral and other customs of this picturesque and rite-observing greenwood.

In an almost purely agricultural county there is perhaps no more appropriate custom than that of the ingathering, or harvest home, and this is a festival observed with due honour in most of the villages of rural Warwickshire. In the early years of the present century the celebrations to Ceres were accompanied by associations of a picturesque and scenic character which now seem to have been discarded for more practical demonstrations. They consisted of humorous and serious duologues between the farmer and his men-servants and maid-servants; they were given in character costume, and were followed by a feast with the usual supply of cakes and ale and the country dance.

On the evening of the day when the last load of grain was safely garnered, the spacious farm kitchens with the wide ingles (which are even yet to be met with in the ancient farmsteads of Shakespeare's greenwood) were prepared for the performance of the duologues. Those taking part in the piece were appropriately clad in costumes typical of the old and new fashioned peasants; the dialogue being taken from "The Husbandman and Serving Man." The performances are thus described by Mr. Scarlett Potter of Halford, near Stratford-on-Avon:

The farmer walks slowly across the stage, leaning on a long and stout staff; the candidate for service steps briskly about, and taps his leg with a light switch which he carries in the hand. The dialogue is started by the farmer.

FARMER.
   Hallo! What countryman are you?

MAN.
   I come from the borders of Bengal (*sic*). My father is a buckram-washer, and my mother is a tinker; and I, being a likely-looking lad, and knowing how to use my paddle—so it's walk, walk, walk!
   [*Struts about stage or kitchen floor.*

FARMER.
> Come all you lads that be for service,
>   Come here, you jolly dogs :
> Who will help me with my harvest,
>   Milk my cows and feed my hogs?
>
> Yonder stands as likely a fellow
>   As ever trod in a leathern shoe,
> Canst thou plough, or canst thou harrow?

MAN.
> Oh yes, master; and I can milk too.

FARMER.
> Here's five pounds in standing wages,
>   Daily well thou shalt be fed,
> With good cabbage, beef, and bacon,
>   Butter-milk, and oaten-bread.
>
> Here's a shilling, take it yarnisht [earnest],
>   And a Thursday thou must come;
> For my servants do all leave me,
>   And my work it must be done.

MAN.
> Thank you, master, for your yarnisht,
>   Thank you, master, for your beer;
> Since your servants do all leave you,
>   Then a Thursday I'll be here!

FARMER [*to audience*].
> Ah! I've hired him; you.

The metrical portion of this dialogue is given in a sort of recitative, a chorus or burden, at the end of each verse being taken up by both the performers. The inversion in the man's answer is a piece of rude wit, the counterpart of which was observed in the Christmas mummeries of Shakespeare's greenwood.

The rustic merriment ended with a feast and dance, and probably with more riotous behaviour than would appear seemly to the present sedate times.

Even now, however, the harvest custom in leafy Warwickshire (especially in the cluster of little villages encircling the birthplace of Shakespeare) is an event of some moment, though shorn of a portion of the picturesque trappings and theatrical effects which characterised the proceedings of fifty years ago.

To-day, if fine weather prevails, the festival of the harvest home is not restricted to the occupants and workers of the farm, but is extended by means of an outdoor demonstration to all the dwellers of the village—so far at least as the first portion of the ceremony is concerned. A case I have in mind, which occurred at a village in the historic Vale of the Red Horse (the property of Lord Willoughby de Broke, who with his lady was present at the ceremony) no longer since than the autumn of 1891, may be regarded as typical of the manner in which it is now customary to observe the celebration in honour of a bountiful harvest in the greenwood of historic Warwickshire.

On a beautifully fine October day, the harvest having been ingathered under most auspicious circumstances, the celebrants met at four o'clock in the afternoon at the Sign of the Swan. There a procession was formed. Farmer Trab and Master Scales were mounted on stout horses, representing the farmer of 1791 and 1891. Flags and banners with harvest mottoes, the village drum and fife band, serving-men carrying sheaves of wheat and barley and beans, a gay farm waggon (drawn by the farmer's dandiest team) laden with vegetables, a rustic bearing a huge loaf of bread upon a pole, a pony-carriage in which was seated the wife of Farmer Trab in the picturesque costume of the end of last century—attended by a cockaded flunkey; these and other items followed behind the farmers of two centuries, making a show not devoid of a certain coloured dignity and quite in harmony with the object and the scene.

Having gone a tour of the village the procession halted in front of the house of the Lord of the Manor, where Farmer Trab doled out bread and cheese to the farm servants from a basket in front of his saddle, and some wine from a wooden bottle slung at his side, much to the amusement of my Lord and my Lady who viewed the proceedings from the steps of the Manor. This done the company returned to the Sign of the Swan to feast at the generous table furnished by the host and to perpetuate the harvest custom "in potations pottle deep" after the usage of Shakespeare's time.

Such is the existing mode of celebrating the ingathering of the corn harvest in the Warwickshire greenwood. It is in striking contrast to the kitchen performance of a century ago; but modern ideas are more expansive now than they were even fifty years since, and although much of the homeliness of former times is lost in the rush of to-day, there is still much that is picturesque and entertaining in the present-day observance of the harvest custom in the villages and hamlets of leafy Warwickshire.

There is perhaps no more curious custom extant in any greenwood than "the Candlelight Auction" for the Warton grazing rights, which it is now proper to describe, as the custom occurs in the month of October immediately subsequent to the commemoration of the harvest home.

Between the Warwickshire villages of Polesworth (in the north of the county), where there is a nunnery, and Atherstone, where there is a field in which the crown of Richard the Third is said to have been hidden after the Battle of Bosworth Field, there is a small hamlet called Warton. At "The Boot" or the "Hatter's Arms" of this village (the two inns which the parish boasts) this quaint custom, dating from the time of George the Third, is annually celebrated. It relates to the letting of certain grazing rights upon the herbage of the roadside and upon the common lands in the parish. The rights are let by auction, and the quaint and picturesque part of the custom is that the whole of the grass has to be sold by candle-light, and the last bidder when the flame burns out is the purchaser.

Each year this peculiar candle-light custom (absolutely confined, so far as is known, to Shakespeare's greenwood) is carried out to the letter in the exact spirit prescribed by the Act of Parliament which provides for it. The road-surveyor of the day performs the duties of auctioneer and is present with candles and book. The latter would doubtless be highly entertaining to the antiquary, inasmuch as it contains the record of these yearly auctions by candle-light from October 1, 1815, to the present time, with the prices realised at each sale. At one time, soon after the institution of the custom (which the Register says was in the days when George the Third was King, but which must surely date from an earlier period), the sale used to realise about £50, but a quarter of that amount is now considered a satisfactory result.

All being ready, the tallow candle (one of the chief "properties" of the scene) is cut into five lengths half an inch high, there being five lots of herbage to be sold; each half-inch of candle being for one lot. Then the road-surveyor auctioneer proceeds to describe the lots. This is highly amusing in its way, for the promotion to the post of honour in the sale usually inspires the road-surveyor with a pretty wit; and he alludes quite gaily to the sporting rights over an old gravel pit and to the pond in Lot I. (which has no fish in it), and concludes with the exhortation, "Get on, gentlemen, please; the light's burning."

But the eyes of the company are attracted to the flame of the candle. It is something to watch, something to make jests upon. And yet the company show not the slightest disposition to bid for the herbage until the candle-light is dying out. Then the competition is remarkably brisk, and at the last flicker of flame the lot is knocked down amid roars of laughter.

Bidders of to-day for the Warton grazing rights, however, are far more decorous than were their prototypes of fifty years ago. The Warwickshire farmers and graziers of the past were a merrier and, mayhap, more riotous set of men than those meeting at the "Hatters' Arms" or "The Boot Inn" to-day; for it is set down in the book that upon some bygone occasions competitors would artfully blow out or otherwise extinguish the flame, and thus create disorder in the auction-room. Still, the candle-light auction of to-day is not less interesting because it is more orderly; and that this curious custom has survived for the best part of a century is a proof of the vitality of the customs of Shakespeare's greenwood.

The custom of the payment of "wroth silver" to the stewards of the Dukes of Buccleuch (Lords of the Manor of Knightlow Hundreds) is one of the most singular and picturesque of all the customs observed in Warwickshire at the present day, and, so far as is known, is now practised in no other English county. There was a similar custom existing in the New Forest in Hampshire in 1670, where "rother" and "cattle money" appear to have been paid by the inhabitants to the owners of different Manors for rights of herbage ; but to-day Shakespeare's greenwood seems to be the only place in England where this relic of early Saxon times is still practised with almost the same curious formalities as those observed at the wroth silver payment of eight centuries ago.

As an example of the growth and longevity of customs when once set in the soil of leafy Warwickshire, this payment of wroth silver custom is probably without parallel in any other English county. It dates, according to Domesday and Dugdale, from the days of King Canute (about the year 1018), who appointed a verderer or chief woodsman—represented by the land steward of to-day—over the forest districts, with powers to act as judge, and whose duties consisted in seeing that no encroachments were made or Royal forest destroyed, to seize robbers frequenting the woods, to cause the destruction of wild animals, to see to the stalling of beasts of venery, and to prevent cattle straying.

This Royal Verderer was vested with authority to hold courts every forty days, or as often as occasion might require, in some convenient place in the neighbourhood ; to punish offenders, to collect fines imposed, and take charge of the King's dues. One verderer was appointed over the forests in a certain district. It is probable that at that early period this chief woodlander had control, not only over the Royal woods, which then existed as the Forest of Arden in Warwickshire, but also over the then greater Forest of Cannock Chase in Staffordshire, and other woodlands in the immediate neighbourhood.

The dwellers in the Forest had certain privileges granted to them in regard to the grazing of the vast unenclosed lands then in existence, and these in course of time they obtained as their rights—often paying acknowledgments to the King or to the Lord of the Manor, either in labour or remuneration in money or in cattle; and to these rights and charges are due the ceremonies of "wroth silver," "wroth money,' "hoctive moneth," "turfdale moneth," and other similar customs; none of which now exist in Shakespeare's greenwood but that chief and most ancient of them all—the payment of "the wroth silver."

On Knightlow Hill (an eminence on the

old London coach road between Coventry and Dunchurch, within the parish of Ryton-on-Dunsmore) the observance of this custom is annually carried out " before sunrise on Martinmas Day." The steward of the Duke of Buccleuch, representatives of the parishes upon which the toll is levied, woodlanders attracted thither by the prospects of a supply of rum and milk, and a few other persons (mostly antiquarians) interested in the practice of this unique Saxon legacy of feudal times, assemble round the base of an old roadside cross which stands upon the brow of an ancient British tumulus or barrow, and in which there is a hollow formed for the reception of the wroth silver. Tolls ranging from one penny halfpenny to two shillings and three pence halfpenny are " called " from twenty-eight parishes in the Hundred of Knightlow; and for non-payment of these fees there is a fine of twenty shillings for every penny not forthcoming, or else the forfeiture of a white bull with a red nose and ears of the same colour.

This curious fine has been once enforced during the past half-century, a white bull having been demanded by the steward of Lord John Scott, of Cawston Lodge, near Dunchurch, the then lord of the manor, in a case where the money either was not paid at all or was not paid before sunrise—the latter being an important point in the observance of the custom. The beast, however, though offered, was rejected because it did not fully answer to the description laid down in the charter.

It would appear to be almost impossible at the present time to find a white bull with a red nose and ears of the same colour; but at the period when the ceremony was first instituted, animals of that kind were very numerous; the bulls of the breed being in such great demand for sport, that stringent laws were passed for their preservation.

The ceremony in its chief points is conducted as follows. The steward takes his stand facing the east and invites those present to form a ring round the cross, whereupon he recites "The Charter of Assembly" commencing, "Wroth Silver collected at Knightlow Cross by the Duke of Buccleuch as Lord of the Manor of the Hundreds of Knightlow."

The parishes liable to the fees are then cited to appear, and each representative of the parish present, upon the calling of the name, casts the required sum into the stone.

The ancient mode of payment was that the person paying must go thrice round the cross saying "The Wroth Silver," and then lay the money in the hole before good witness; for if not duly performed the parishes were liable to the fine. These formalities have but slightly changed through the eight centuries of their observance; the custom of to-day being that the person does not walk thrice round the cross, but simply throws the money into the hollow of the stone, calling out "Wroth Silver" as each separate amount falls in; the money being afterwards gathered, in single payments, into the hand of the bailiff.

Without doubt there is no more picturesque custom extant to-day in the greenwood of any English county than the custom of the payment of wroth silver at the cross of the tumulus on Knightlow Hill. The hour of meeting (before sunrise on Martinmas morn), sometimes at a dark daybreak when the celebrants look like shadows moving in the darker shadow of the Hill; the curious nature of the ceremony, and the subsequent breakfast at the "Shoulder of Mutton," at Stretton-on-Dunsmore, where the health of the Duke of Buccleuch ("The Lord of Knightlow Hundreds") is drunk in the time-honoured glasses of rum and milk, form together a picture of country life so quaint and out-of-the-way as to make it quite unique among the customs not only of Shakespeare's greenwood, but of the whole of rural England.

In an evergreen country where the birth of each new child is signalised by the pressing of a "silver bit" into its little pink fist "for luck," it is not surprising that the advent of Christmas Day, when the Redeemer of the world was brought forth and cradled in a manger, should be a time of special rejoicing and of special observance of rites and customs —interesting and picturesque and hoary with the traditions of years.

When the unique custom of the payment of wroth silver before sunrise on Martinmas morning (November 11) is concluded, the peasants of Shakespeare's greenwood descend the weird sides of Knightlow Hill with the knowledge that for at least a month there will be no more out-of-door customs to observe; nothing to delight the hearts of rustic children until December 21st, when (on St. Thomas's Day) they prepare to go " a-Thomasin "; nothing, indeed, to lighten the lives of children of a larger growth until the arrival of Yule-tide, when, in the words of the homely jingle, often heard in the mouths of the Warwickshire farm-hands:

*A Christmas gambol oft can cheer
The poor man's heart through half the year.*

The first signs of the approaching custom of keeping Christmas may be observed as early as the middle of October in the parlour of many a rustic cot in leafy Warwickshire. In the wide and warm ingle-nook a small pyramid of sawn logwood may be seen standing to dry; and in the middle of the room, or in a recess, the great green or yellow marrow is suspended by gay-coloured ribbons from a hook in the rafter—the recipient of many admiring glances, and many wishes for a slice out of it when it shall be served as a Christmas dish.

As the stuffed chine of pork is, among the peasants of this woodland, the customary sign observed at the Mothering, so the showy-ribboned marrow is one of the symbols of the Christmas customs. The marrow is grown to a giant size (the larger the more honour to the grower and the more plentiful the feast), is hung up in the house-parlour until the eve of the festival, and is then prepared and stuffed, and makes, in sober truth, a goodly furnishing for the table and the interiors of those who partake of " a shive."

Another custom, preparatory to the great feast of the year, observed by the secluded dwellers in Shakespeare's greenwood, is the gathering of crabs and the stewing of them for a winter dish. In this we have an ancient custom handed down for at least three hundred years, and in use at the end of the nineteenth century—a fact which seems to show how sacredly some of the old customs are preserved and perpetuated by native-born people of leafy Warwickshire.

Shakespeare was evidently well acquainted with the crab-lore of his own woodland, for not only does he make Caliban say in "The Tempest" (Act II. scene 2),

> *Let me bring thee where crabs grow,*

but in the well-known lines in "Love's Labour's Lost" (Act V. scene 2),

> *When roasted crabs hiss in the bowl,*
> *Then nightly sings the staring owl,*
> *To-who;*
> *To-whit, to-who, a merry note,*
> *While greasy Joan doth keel the pot,*

he alludes to this very dish, the annual making of which is a welcome custom to many a rustic housewife in the poet's own neighbourhood to this day.

Plunged into a dish of cooked sago the roasted crab (well done and nicely sugared) is incomparable eating. Sometimes stewed pears, perry pears for choice, are substituted for crabs when the latter are not forthcoming owing to the depredations of the young rustics; and I well remember staying in a cottage in an isolated village one week in

October when the ancient dame (upright as a poplar though nearly eighty years of age) had so much faith in this Shakespearean dish that the hissing bowl was brought to table most evenings about the time when the staring owl would be singing his nightly song. Thus we have at the fag end of a prosaic century the representation of a custom as poetic as the verse in which it is immortalised.

The custom of the Thomasing, though not now (in its old state) so prevalent as formerly in the out-of-the-way villages and hamlets of Shakespeare's greenwood, is still in extensive use under a new guise, and under newer methods. "Goin' a-Thomasin'" is literally going begging for Christmas gifts, and in the older days (before railways gave such irresistible facilities for the rush to town), when the rustics of Warwickshire, immured in their own woodland, were more stationary than at present, the Thomasing was a custom at once pretty and touching—revealing the fact that even in the core of Nature's heart, far from the madding crowd, the coming of Christmas was indeed the time of Peace and Goodwill towards men.

Similar in design to the custom of the Maying, the rule at the Thomasing (which, as it name implies, was always observed on St. Thomas's Day) was to make a circuit of the villages in procession, and with a little rustic song at the door of cottage, farm, and hall to bring the greetings of the festive season to the inmates, and to plead for gifts with which to "keep Christmas"; a plea which was, and is, seldom disregarded by the kind-hearted farmers and country people, despite contrary seasons and increased rates.

In doing this, too, the better-class folk are simply giving effect to a custom which has been honoured in leafy Warwickshire for hundreds of years, and was especially observed at Stoneleigh (that Liberty Hall of the county) by Humphrey How, the good porter to Thomas, first Lord Leigh; who, after having for years given the bounty of his lord to the poorer dwellers of the greenwood (there were woods indeed at Stoneleigh in those days), at the Thomasing and other times, departed this life on February 6, 1688, leaving the following quaint and touching record of his memory in an inscription tablet on the south wall of Stoneleigh Church:

> *Here lies a faithful friend unto the poor,*
> *Who dealt large alms out of his Lordship's store,*
> *Weep not poor people though your servant's dead,*
> *The Lord himself will give you daily bread.*
> *If markets rise rail not against the rates,*
> *The price is still the same at Stoneleigh Gates.*

Perhaps the prettiest part of the custom which is now synonymous with the old Thomasing is that in which the homely carols are sung at the doors of the larger village houses. In the silence of the dark greenwood (for the carolling is chiefly performed at night) the voices of the singers, many of whom are choristers of the parish church, sound peculiarly attractive, and the very quaintness of the rhymes and the tunes, which are invariably of their own making, often enhance the effect of the carols

One Christmas a few years since I heard the carollists raising their voices through the dim and silent greenwood, and caught the words of their rhymes, which were as follows —sung to a swinging, swaying tune, which, owing to the scene and time, had something sweet yet strange about it.

> *Little Cock Robin sat on a wall,*
> *We wish you a Merry Christmas*
> *And a great snowfall;*
> *Apples to eat*
> *And nuts to crack,*
> *We wish you a Merry Christmas*
> *With a rap, tap, tap.*

With a repetition of the "rap, tap, tap" of the song the doors of the houses were knocked at, and the plea for Christmas gifts made and responded to with that good feeling invariably characteristic of the well-to-do people of the in-Arden villages of Warwickshire; many of whom delight to perpetuate the simple customs of rustic life, which are often the only variations in the existence of these hemmed-in woodlanders. Their gifts secured by the choristers, the dark and sleepy landscape rings with the verses of the beautiful Christmas hymn, "While Shepherds Watched their Flocks by Night," given as a sort of thank-offering for value received; and then relapses once more into its usual quietude.

As it was formerly the custom at the ingathering of the corn harvest to commemorate the event by duologues in costume, so at the Christmas feast in each year a band of Warwickshire peasants was wont to appear in the farmsteads and perform various acts of mummery to the assembled guests. The mask and the mummer, however, are now seen only at rare intervals in the farm kitchen; and what in the past was a decidedly picturesque entertainment, formed and carried out by the humbler folk for the delectation of their betters, has now been taken up by the betters themselves, and in "The Hall" of most villages in Shakespeare's greenwood it is the custom to organise theatricals and pieces of mummery and perform them from Christmas Day until Twelfth Night.

By its translation to the Hall of the well-to-do, the Christmas mumming has lost its chiefest charm; for of all the customs observed in this classic woodland none could have been more picturesque than this—the masked mummer bursting out of the darkness of the sheep-fold into the spacious farm kitchen, where the flaming yule-log in the ingle was making the shadows dance hornpipes upon the walls and floor. There is very little doubt that the Warwickshire mumming of centuries ago gave Shakespeare the text for those incomparable scenes in "A Midsummer Night's Dream," in which Bottom the weaver is the chief mummer.

Though their mummeries are now emasculated to a condition in which picturesque Nature takes little part, the rustics of Shakespeare's greenwood still number among their customs the venerable one of bringing in the Yule-log. It would be surprising if it were not so in a country where the sered and wasting remnants of the ancient Forest of Arden stand around in such abundance—ready grown for the axe and the hand of the woodlander. The peasant for his cottage parlour, the farmer for his spacious kitchen, and the squire for his stately hall, vie with one another in securing the largest, the firmest, and the driest log for the Christmas hearthstone—each according to his requirements and the size of the fireplace in their respective domiciles.

With the humbler true-born native of Shakespeare's greenwood, whose mind is still overlaid with a cloudy texture of superstition, any wood will do for the Yule-log but the wood of the wych-elm. This must never be burnt in the house for fear " the old 'ooman " who is supposed to inhabit that tree should come down in vengeance upon those who dare to desecrate her branches. It used to be the custom to preserve a piece of the previous year's brand with which to light the log, and in connection with this there is a rhyme, often repeated, which says :

> *Kindle the Christmas brand and then*
> *Till sunrise let it burn ;*
> *Which quenched, then lay it up agen*
> *Till Christmas next return.*
>
> *Part must be kept wherewith to tend*
> *The Christmas log next year ;*
> *And when 'tis safely kept, the fiend*
> *Can do no mischief there.*

Among the rustic housewives of leafy Warwickshire it has been the custom from time immemorial to make use of the fruits of Nature, and to this day, despite the cheapness of wines, the berries of the elder trees (which in this neighbourhood usually show a wonderful harvest) are pressed into service by the neat-handed Phyllises of the villages and a wine made therefrom which is but little inferior to port of a good vintage. The wine is bottled or kegged and left for some time (often for years) to mature, and is invariably brought out on the morning of Christmas Day, heated and sugared to the taste of the sampler, and taken with hot toast.

This is one of the Christmas customs of Shakespeare's greenwood which at the present time is not so greatly in vogue as in the days of the Squire Cass of George Eliot's "Silas Marner," who drank a flagon of ale for breakfast; though in many isolated cots by the wood or on a waste, the drinking of glasses of elder wine is observed with unfailing regularity; and if the morning be winterly, it is a cheering cup for Dick, the shepherd, and other out-of-door workers, when they come home to breakfast in the warm farm kitchen.

That this custom was observed by all classes alike, lay and clerical, in the early years of the present century may be taken for granted since it was practised by the celebrated divine, Dr. Samuel Parr, the classical parson of Hatton, near Warwick, who, in a letter to a friend at Norwich, remarked ; " I gave some rum to the farmers' wives, and some vidonia and elder wine to their daughters ; and the lads and lasses had a merry dance in the large schoolroom"—a pleasant picture of country life in Warwickshire some seventy odd years ago.

In connection with these Christmas customs there are two curious observances among the more secluded dwellers of Shakespeare's greenwood, which, though they partake of the nature of superstitions, may very well be allowed a record here. They both occur on Christmas Eve, just upon the stroke of twelve (the witching hour), when the occupants of cot or farmstead, in the one instance, troop down the rustic garden to the beehives, " to hear the bees sing their Christmas carols." The belief is that these busy insects are as pleased at the birth of a new Christmas Day as the members of the human family, and testify their mirth by singing a set of new carols for the occasion. It is certainly a pretty and poetical custom which draws the peasants into the dim garden at midnight on Christmas Eve in the simple faith that the bees are singing Christmas in.

The other superstitious custom is perhaps even more singular and gives a well-defined silhouette, as it were, of the picturesque character of the peasants of Shakespeare's greenwood. They believe that wild nature as well as human nature is profoundly grateful for the benefits conferred upon the world by the birth of the Redeemer; and with the dark, early dawn of each Christmas morn (immediately upon the first stroke of twelve), the gentle shepherds aver that the cattle in the fields—the sheep, cows, horses, and asses—reverentially kneel with their faces towards the east, and remain in that position until the clock of the village church has proclaimed the fact that another Christmas Day is born.

With the passing of the Christmas festivities and the arrival of New Year's Eve, the musical rustics of leafy Warwickshire again go in procession to the doors of the village houses and sing their greetings (in the dark and stilly night) to the occupants of cottage, farm, and hall. If only on account of the quaintness of their rhymes, the custom of "Singing the New Year in" deserves to be preserved, and some record kept of the lines used for the occasion; especially so as there is a likelihood that it may become rarer each year. For five years I have not heard the choristers singing their New Year's greetings, but on New Year's Eve in 1893 I chanced to be out on the edge of a village, and came upon a group trilling the following quaint lines:

The roads are very dirty,
   My boots are very thin,
I have a little pocket
   To put a penny in.
     God send you happy
     God send you happy,
Praise the Lord to send you all
   A Happy New Year.

God bless the master of this house,
   God bless the mistress true,
And all the little children
   Around the table too.
     And send you A Happy New Year,
     And send you A Happy New Year.
God bless you all,
   Both great and small,
And send you A Happy New Year.

Sung in the last hour of the last day in the year, and in the silence of a dim green world where men thin away to the utmost insignificance, these quaint and homely lines of blessing for friend and neighbour (sung in a befitting minor key) form an appropriate ending to the year's customs of Shakespeare's greenwood; a country so rich in historic and poetic associations, in traditions, in natural science, in folk-lore, customs, and dialect, that turn which ever way you will something new and interesting is invariably to be found. But when it is remembered that for forty years Robert Dover, of Barton-on-the-Heath, Warwickshire (a native of Shakespeare's greenwood), was the chief director of the celebrated games on the Cotswold Hills, it is, perhaps, not surprising that so many customs of interest and rarity should still be observed in the secluded hamlets of leafy Warwickshire.

The Folk-Lore

The Horse's White Foot.—The Robin's Song.—The Sky-Signs.—The Fleecy Barometer.—Rain Signs.—The Bee Hives.—Telling the Bees.—The Swarming of Bees.—Catching Ascension Day Rain.—The Oak and the Ash Proverb.—The Fern-Seed Love Charm.—Moon Signs.—The Magpie and the Ark.—Cheeses and Sneezes.—The Stranger in the Teacup.—The Stranger on the Grate.—The Spark in the Candle-Flame.—The Burnt Milk.—Egg-Shells and Laying Hens.—The Turkey's Gobble.—The Tree-Cure for Rickets.—Passing through the Cleft.—Ring-Finger.—The Baby's Birthday.—Lucky Birthdays.—Death and the Open Door.—The Sage Tree and the Master.—The Whistling Woman.

The Folk-Lore*

ISOLATED in his own greenery, far from the busy haunts where men most do congregate, the peasant of rural Warwickshire is essentially prone to a belief in marks, signs, and other outward observances; and treasures up with a quite picturesque conviction (with a faith worthy of a better cause) the heirlooms of folk-lore which have devolved upon him from bygone generations.

* These examples of folk-lore are not necessarily confined to Warwickshire, though the district as a whole has preserved bygone beliefs and ideas more tenaciously than most parts of rural England.

If a Warwickshire farmer were in need of a new horse and made his want known among those with horses to sell; and if accordingly a fine black horse with one white foot were brought for his inspection, his eye would at once alight upon the white foot and he would be sure to shake his head and say:

> *One white foot is bad, and two are too many,*
> *That horse is best that does not have any.*

This is an example of the folk-lore of Shakespeare's greenwood, an influence which is as tenacious of life in the mind of the Warwickshire countryman as the idiom of his own tongue. All the signs, small and great, that are seen in field, lane, woodland, or on hill in this classic county are made a note of by the dwellers therein, and turned to use in their everyday life.

Any one who moves among the inhabitants of this neighbourhood when in the open will be surprised and interested at the many quaint observances of the so-called " common people." The people, indeed, may be un-lettered and common in the sense that they work and live by the sweat of their brow, and are by no means fastidious in the matter of dress, but their way of looking at things and their manner of doing them are, without question, uncommon, if not curious and poetical.

The small pipings of the robin, which would have no effect whatever on the average townsman, are full of omen to the Warwickshire ploughman driving his team of horses merrily afield. To him the robin is both sacred and melancholy. The most uncultured of clowns will hesitate to do harm to the bird with ruby breast, for with him the robin is a weather harbinger. If it sings in the morning there will surely be rain before night; if the pensive fellow pipes at sundown it will be a fine day to-morrow.

The redbreast is a sacred bird. I have known Warwickshire rustic boys, with the true seeds of religious feeling common to the dwellers in this famous greenwood working within them, even to decline on their bird's-nesting expeditions to rob the nest of the robin. The reason is that the robin is God's bird with them. In their simple faith the robin was the attendant of Jesus at the Crucifixion, and crimsoned its breast in ministering to His needs. Thus the robin (with the wren) is a sacred bird, the peasant's feeling finding expression in the quaint couplet:

*The robin and the wren
Are God's cock and hen.*

Having in view the legendary ministrations of the robin, it is quite in accord with the circumstances of the case that the peasants of Shakespeare's greenwood should regard it as a melancholy bird. Its duties at the Cross and the scenes it saw there were of a character to sadden its whole life; and so with these sequestered rustics it is the bird of sorrow. The influence of Shakespeare may have something to do with the holding of this popular belief, for the immortal poet himself addresses to the robin the question,

How now, Robin, art thou melancholy?

As they that go down to the sea in ships and occupy their business in great waters see the wonders of Nature on the deep, so the shepherd, who goes down to his fold in a coomb of the hills at all hours of the day and night, beholds the mysteries of Nature on land. The shepherd of this greenwood is as full of folk-lore of all kinds as a good ear of wheat is full of grain. His glance at the sky is the glance of a reading man ; it is his book in which he reads the signs which portend good or ill to his flocks and herds.

The ancient pastoral jingle, recited by rustics in every village of Warwickshire when the signs appear,

> *A red sky in the morning*
> *Is the shepherd's warning :*
> *A red sky at night*
> *Is the shepherd's delight,*

is the gospel of the keeper of sheep in this neighbourhood. A burning red flush arching the sky in the morning will prevent him from tarrying over creature comforts ; and not until his young lambs are well under cover in the great red barns, or he has lent a hand in spreading the tar cloths over the wheat ricks, will he be induced to return to breakfast. But a similar scarlet flush at night, covering the top of the coomb like a rosy canopy, will take him on his homeward way leisurely, for in his familiar belief that red sign surely foretells a bright day on the morrow.

If those morning and evening sky-signs are sometimes lacking in their appearance, the faith in his own flock as a barometer of the workings of Nature are always present in the mind of the man of fleece. He reads their movements and moods as he studies the lights and shadows of the sky, and has an abiding conviction of their truth.

> *When sheep do huddle by tree and bush,*
> *Bad weather is coming with wind and slush ;*

and when the shepherd of Shakespeare's greenwood observes his flock huddling together under tree or hedge, he at once accepts the sign and takes measures accordingly—never for a moment doubting the accuracy of his fleecy barometer.

The folk-lore, indeed, pertaining to atmospheric changes in leafy Warwickshire is of a very full and quaint character. This is no doubt accounted for by the fact that the bulk of the people in the entirely rural districts are field-workers, are out in the open late and early, and in all seasons, and thus take note of the natural signs that appear in the sky and on landscape; which have gone some way towards founding a literature of their own—mostly a literature of simple rhymes.

> *If it rains before seven*
> *'Twill be fine before eleven,*

is a prophecy which the true-born native never thinks of disbelieving, though it is not always realised by the actual turn of events. Another popular belief in the same category is that if it rains all morning and stops before twelve, the rest of the day will be fine; if on the other hand, rain begins to fall just after noon, then the whole of the rest part of the day will be wet. The latter "fore-token," as it is called, is regarded as quite infallible by the peasantry of this greenwood, who will confidently resume work again if the rain ceases by half-past twelve, and forego their labour if it begins at that time.

Perhaps the most curious evidences of the union which exists between natural and human life in the rural districts of Warwickshire are to be found in connection with the folk-lore of bees. Shakespeare's greenwood has for a long period been a great honey-producing district. Few gardens of the scattered cots in village or hamlet are to be seen without at least one hive of bees; and there was one, to my own knowledge, which had no less than one hundred hives. Many of these hives are home-made (the work of the ingenious hands of the rustic), and of the quaintest designs as well as the most ambitious; two I once saw in a garden of old-fashioned flowers at Lillington being made of pure white oyster-shells, and were exact reproductions of the famous Warwick Castle.

What charm or influence bees have upon the affairs of the human family is a subject as interesting as it is undeterminable; but there is no doubt or obscurity about the fact that no prudent cottager of leafy Warwickshire ever omits to take the bees into his confidence. The small honey-gatherers, indeed, in spite of their minute size in comparison with the size of their keepers, exercise quite a despotic power over them. They insist upon being "told" everything, and there is a popular belief that if the bees are not informed of all the leading occurrences in the family some visitations of ill-luck are sure to follow.

Thus the business of "telling the bees" of any important event happening in the homestead is never forgotten, or dreamt of being omitted. The bees must be told of a birth, marriage, departure, return, or death of any member of the keeper's family, and then all goes well; but let this ceremony be once omitted (either from forgetfulness, neglect, or design), then a penalty in some form or other will have to be paid. Such is the steadfast faith of the Warwickshire rustics, who, to avoid the penalty, tell their bees everything.

In regard to the swarming of bees there is a very popular rhyming augury in use in all the villages of rural Warwickshire. In it the value of the different months of the year in which the swarms occur are faithfully laid down in the following manner:

> *A swarm of bees in May*
> *Is worth a load of hay.*
> *A swarm of bees in June*
> *Is worth a silver spoon.*
> *A swarm of bees in July*
> *Is not worth a butterfly.*

The influence of these prognostications is seen in the interest shown by country dwellers in this neighbourhood when their bees swarm in May; whereas later swarms worth, according to the lore of the subject, but a silver spoon and a butterfly, occasion only a mild enthusiasm among the occupants of cottage or farmstead.

In concluding these brief examples of the folk-lore attaching to bees existent in the Warwickshire greenwood, I may mention that in connection with the ceremony of "telling the bees" there is one belief held more strongly than many others, and that is that if, when the master of the house dies, the bees are not told of the event, they will leave the hive in a body and go right away.

A very curious open-air practice still widely prevalent among older inhabitants of village and hamlet in out-of-the-way places, is the catching of falling rain on Ascension Day. This practice was observed by almost all the natives in the days when home-made bread was the rule in every village homestead; and to-day in those cottages where bread is still made and baked at home the rain-water which fell on Ascension Day is brought out for use. The belief is that rain falling on that day, if caught and bottled and used with the leaven (a teaspoonful at a time), is a sure preventative against "heavy bread." Accordingly when it happened to rain upon that auspicious day vessels were held out, the rain was caught and bottled, and used as circumstances might require, in the full and firm conviction that batches of "light" bread would result from mixing it with the leaven.

Observing the moods, signs, and aspects of Nature enabled the peasants of Shakespeare's greenwood in bygone days to frame many of the old fore-tokens and beliefs which have now such a hold upon the occupants of the dab-and-wattle and thatch-roofed cottages. The many prophecies concerning the bursting of the leaf are now implicitly believed in; that one having reference to the ash and the oak being still, through years of time and observance, become quite a proverb in the belief of the rural dwellers.

In woody Warwickshire there appear to be two versions of the prognostication. Both are in rhyme, and both are in extensive use;

yet, strange to relate, each seems to give quite a different prophecy in respect to the ash preceding the oak. The one most chiefly used runs as follows:

> *If the oak comes out before the ash,*
> *We shall have a summer of splash;*
> *If the ash comes out before the oak,*
> *We shall have a summer of smoke.*

A summer of smoke means to the native a hot, dry summer, with steaming pastures in the mornings and smoking herbage during the day, which reads strangely when considered side by side with the other prophecy:

> *If the oak comes out before the ash,*
> *We shall have but a little splash;*
> *If the ash comes out before the oak,*
> *We shall have a downright soak.*

A downright soak seems to signify a summer of rain rather than a summer of smoke, but this latter prognostication is the older of the two, and the experience of modern country-folk in this woodland goes to show that atmospheric changes have reversed the order of the proverbs, and that now when the leafage of the ash precedes that of the

oak, a hot, dry ...
smoke") is the inva...
 The folk-lore pre...
greenwood relating to ...
moon is both extensi...
There is first of all a stea...
wise woman of the village...
collection of domiciles wh...
title of village or hamlet ... wise
woman") culls her simples b... ...e light of
the moon, otherwise no virtue attaches to
them. The maiden, too, when sowing the
fern seed which she gathered for her love-
charm on Midsummer Day must sow the
seed by moonlight, and repeat as she scatters
it:

Fern seed I sow, fern seed I hoe,
In hopes my true love will come after me and mow,

or else she will not attain her heart's desire.
 In all matters relating to the moon the
greatest good follows the doing of the correct
thing. When the first new moon of the year
makes its appearance it is the correct thing for
every countryman of leafy Warwickshire, when
seeing it for the first time, to bow to it nine

times to secure good luck for the coming year. The men-folk have to bow one hundred and eight times during the year, and the women-folk have to curtsy the same number of times; for the first moon of each lunar month exacts nine bows and nine curtsies from each man and woman as the homage to be paid for the good luck which this moon-worship is believed to give. It is also a common practice to turn the money in the pocket when each succeeding new moon is seen for the first time.

One of the surest signs of fair weather is, in the belief of the Warwickshire rustic, connected with the appearance of the moon. When the moon sits perfectly stagnant in the sky, with her horns pointing upward, when, as Martin Poyser says in "Adam Bede" (chapter xviii. page 159), "it lies like a boat," there is never likely to be any rain for some little time. "There's many sines as is false," continues Poyser, "but that's sure"; and certainly the peasants of Shakespeare's greenwood have an invincible faith in that sign. The prognostication for rain among these country dwellers is when the crescent moon stands downward, when, in fact, the boat figure is reversed. It is then believed that the moon is so tilted that the rain will run out at the horns.

In spots so far from the madding crowd as some of the isolated little hamlets of rural Warwickshire it is but natural that the magpie, "the Mag," as it is called by the rustics, should be a famous augur. The rooks talk among the undulations, and "go to school" in the basins of the landscapes; but "the Mag" is far more knowing than the rook, and it must be confessed that the peasants of this greenwood, if not a little afraid of him, are always anxious to conciliate him. There is a strange belief amongst them that the magpie was the only bird out of all the birds of the air who refused to enter the Ark of Noah, preferring to sit on the roof and enjoy the scene of the Deluge. Thus "the Mag" is a curious bird, has a talent for spying out things, and is believed to have the power of inflicting sorrow upon those who behold it singly, and good luck when seen in twos, threes, and fours.

Among people of poetic instincts, such as the dwellers in Shakespeare's greenwood (who were born and have lived all their lives in the haunts of Nature, far from the hum and bustle of crowded towns and cities) the belief in occurrences, moods, and signs, which the average townsman would pass over almost without notice, is so strong as to be a trait of character as peculiar to them as their manners, language, and customs.

The out-of-door examples of folk-lore, as might be expected in a people who spend the greater half of their lives in the open air, are numerous, picturesque, and poetical; but the indoor practices and beliefs are no less prevalent, and by their quaintness, allied with the obscurity of their origin, are sometimes more interesting than the out-of-door, and frequently more poetical.

In many parts of leafy Warwickshire cheeses are made with almost as much success as butter. It is an important home industry among the more prosperous of the farm folk, and particular attention is paid to it. Neat-handed Phyllis, however, must have one qualification more strongly marked than any other, or else the cheeses will not prove satisfactory to the maker or the partaker—she must not sneeze. There is much humour in the greenwood rhyme which proscribes any woman who sneezes or takes snuff from having a hand in the cheese-making. It is as follows:

> *A woman who sneezes*
> *Ought not to make cheeses,*
> *Or ever take snuff.*
> *Put her hands in a muff.*

The injunction is well intended and wise with regard to the taking of snuff, inasmuch as the woman who does take snuff must invariably be the woman who sneezes, and neither the snuff nor the attendant sneeze are desirable qualifications in the maker of cheeses.

The sneeze, however, has a certain lore attached to it among the peasants of Shakespeare's greenwood which for them is full of significance. Every day upon which the sneeze occurs the occasion is noted, and those who hear it proclaim its import. In like manner the number of sneezes is taken into account, and their meaning proclaimed with a serious or cheerful face as the case may be, according to the number of sneezes; which denote various things, such as being or going to be pleased, crossed, angry, kissed, in safety or danger, going to receive a letter, and other similar occurrences, finally winding up with a proposal of marriage.

In respect of the day of the sneeze, the Warwickshire jingle is very precise, and is implicitly believed in by every native born in the greenwood.

> *Sneeze on Monday, sneeze for danger ;*
> *Sneeze on Tuesday, kiss a stranger ;*
> *Sneeze on Wednesday, have a letter ;*
> *Sneeze on Thursday, something better ;*
> *Sneeze on Friday, sneeze for sorrow ;*
> *Sneeze on Saturday, see true-love to-morrow.*

Nothing is mentioned in the rhyme of the effect of a sneeze on Sunday, but the belief is that a sneeze on that day means a visit from the Parson on Monday. "There now, Parson Wordington will be coming to see us to-morrow," is the exclamation most likely to follow a Sunday sneeze in the cottage of a Warwickshire rustic, and the rooms are set in order for the approaching visitor.

The forecasts of approaching visitors are,

indeed, very numerous and generally believed in. Their signs appear in the morning tea-cup, and in the nightly candle that takes the woodlanders to bed; and the curious point of interest is, that the signs are not merely noticed when they come into view, but are eagerly, even anxiously looked for, especially by the maidens, who invariably have their minds overlaid with a veil of romantic non-sense.

It is the first dreg that appears on the surface of the tea that foretells the advent of the stranger. This is carefully rescued by the aid of a teaspoon and pinched between the fingers to ascertain its sex. If soft, it is a sign that the visitor will be a lady; if hard, it is perfectly sure to be a gentlemen. The red-hot speck or star in the flame of the candle denotes the coming of a stranger on the morrow, but gives no clue to the sex. It is nevertheless believed in by the dwellers of this romantic greenwood even more implicitly than the sign in the tea-cup, and upon seeing it the good housewife never neglects to put her house " to rights."

That spark in the candle is a great delight

to the Warwickshire lass in love. To her it means a letter from her true love of course. In the words of the rhyme connected with the foretoken,

> *A spark in the wick*
> *Brings a love-letter quick.*

As soon as the damsel sees it she will run across to the candlestick to find out whether the letter is posted. This is done by lifting the candlestick gently in the air and bringing it down upon the table again with a smart little bang. If the star falls (as it invariably does from the effect of the concussion), the letter is already posted, and the rustic beauty goes to bed with the firm conviction that she will receive a billet-doux from her lover in the morning. There is quite a poetical and Shakespearean flavour about this example of folk-lore which might well have been extant in the poet's own days.

There is another similar and much-used form of fore-knowing the arrival of a visitor in vogue among the peasants of Shakespeare's greenwood, and that is the appearance of the thin black leaf, or film, of coal which is sometimes seen flickering upon the bars of the grate. This with them is a sure sign of the impending visit of some one, stranger or friend.

"There be a stranger on the grate yon," is a remark which will act as the signal for a general rush to the grate to discover whether the visitor is coming on foot or in a carriage. The performance is accomplished by bending down in front of the fire and clapping the hands before "the stranger." If the filmy leaf leaps back into the fire, the visitor is coming on wheels (that is, in a carriage)—in fact, has already started ; if it falls out on to the hearthstone the stranger is coming thither on foot. This is the belief and affirmation of the country dwellers in this leafy neighbourhood, and the stranger on the grate is watched for by them with a more than common interest.

In a country so pastoral as rural Warwickshire it is a matter for no surprise that simple beliefs in connection with the farm stock are very prevalent with the natives. The origin of these beliefs is frequently shrouded in mystery, but the formalities are still held sacred, and though they may be retained in some cases with an eye to material advantage, that does not in the least diminish their interest. Among the farmer's wives, who are chiefly more frugal and careful than the men themselves, the belief that if the milk is burnt in the boiling the cows will run dry, is held in such good faith that the pot is invariably watched, notwithstanding the ancient housewife's dictum that

The watched pot never boils.

The Warwickshire poultry-maid, too, will take good care of the egg-shells. It is not accounted good luck to keep the shells in the house, and they are taken away as soon as may be convenient ; but if by any mischance some person, unacquainted with the folk-lore of the subject, should burn the egg-shells, then, in the rustic belief the hens will cease laying. Where this faith is the strongest is in the isolated homesteads on the waste or by the side of a wood, and there the utmost care is taken to prevent any single egg-shell being thrown into the fire, so that the fecundity of the hens may not be stayed.

In connection with the folk-lore of farm stock it is nothing short of remarkable to notice how keen and minute is the observation of the native-grown rustic, and how rich in beliefs, for him, are the many signs that he sees. Nothing escapes his attention. The smallest and most trifling incidents in the eyes of the townsman are to the rustic of Shakespeare's greenwood signs sometimes fraught with the deepest significance. When the turkeys make that weird noise in their throats known as "gobbling," the farmer or poultry herd observes the sign at once and takes measures accordingly. The gobble of the turkey is in their simple faith a sign of a change in atmospheric conditions, a change for the worse—the coming, in short, of foul weather.

If there happens to be a stranger or visitor in the house the gobble of the turkeys will keep him there a spell longer than it was his intention to stay, through the representations of the farmer that a storm is coming on. There is an allusion to this belief in the old Warwickshire rhyme so often quoted by the ancient ones of the village :

When the wind is east and turkeys gobble,
It is no time a horse to hobble ;
But let him range to catch the breeze
Should he be troubled with the heaves.

The troubles of the flesh in both man and beast have their remedies in the folk-lore of the country. Indeed, there is, perhaps, no stronger, keener, or more permanent belief in the minds of the Warwickshire peasants than that of the virtue of tree and herb as cures for the ills of animate Nature. This is an ancient faith, prevalent in Shakespeare's days, and well known to the poet himself, who finely describes the weedy and tattered man (or woman) wandering in the lush meads, or by the Avon's classic side,

Culling of simples ;

and among the more isolated dwellers of to-day, who are, for the most part, as stationary as the trees in their own greenwood, the belief in Nature's own remedies for Nature's ailments is as firmly held as it was in the time of Shakespeare, in spite of the ever-growing army, even in country places, of professors of medicine ; who, however, use less picturesque arts than those of the Warwickshire rustics.

One curious practice still largely employed in out-of-the-way districts of this neighbourhood, is that known as "the tree cure," in the efficacy of which the natives hold an unslayable faith. Any weak child (but more especially those suffering with the rickets) is a proper subject for the tree cure. The child is brought to the foot of a twin ash, or, better still, to a tree with a cleft in it, and is then passed through the cleft by those in charge of it, in the full and firm conviction that his contact with the tree will strengthen him and cause his bones to go together and set hard.

Many a weird-looking Warwickshire peasant who has outwitted Time for twenty years, and who is as tough and gnarled and crooked as the old codlin in his own garden, will point to the tree through whose cleft he was drawn in his childhood, and will tell you that he would not have been here now if he "had'na bin passed through the cleft yon." This belief in the tree cure, indeed, is as strongly held now as it is ancient and romantic, and a part of the folk-lore rite in connection therewith is that the welfare of the infant depends to a great extent upon the preservation of the tree.

To preserve the twin, or double, ash, and the tree with a riven trunk, is therefore the subject of special care to those who are associated with them by means of the cure; for it is a proverb among the rustics of this greenwood that when the tree falls it is the signal for the fall of the life that in its early stages was passed through the cleft.

Beginning thus with the early days of life it is no wonder that the folk-lore of Shakespeare's greenwood continues in the belief of the peasants until the sands of Time have run out their last grain. The infant when passed through the cleft in the tree is, perhaps, too young to have a clear perception of the meaning of the rite; but when the children have grown to a thinking age, they enter as simply and faithfully into the practices of their woodland as the older dwellers from whom they inherit their observances and beliefs.

Any one passing through one of the sequestered hamlets of woody Warwickshire, and through a group of boy and girl villagers which is invariably to be met with there (for where the voices of the cuckoo and the corn-crake are heard there also will be heard the voices of the children), may often have the evidence of the child's knowledge of the folk-lore of its neighbourhood brought directly under his notice. One child will promise another to do a certain thing, and will ratify the promise by linking its little finger with the little finger of his or her friend, while rehearsing the words,

*Ring finger, blue bell,
Tell a lie and go to hell,*

which are certainly more familiar in the mouth of a Warwickshire child than many others in its own language.

There is a probability that this poetic method of enforcing the truth of an uttered sentiment dates from the days of Shakespeare, and may have been observed by the young poet himself when making his promise to marry Anne Hathaway in the groves of hidden Shottery, for there is an allusion in one of his plays to a similar observance:

where, in the First Part of "King Henry the Fourth (Act. II. scene 3), Lady Percy addresses her husband, Hotspur, as follows :

*In faith I'll break thy little finger, Harry,
An if thou wilt not tell me all things true.*

The fate of a child is a subject which in the folk-lore of the Warwickshire peasant-mother seems to have a special significance. It must be born upon a certain day of the week to bring joy to her heart; and so strong is the belief of the average rustic woman in the luck or ill-luck which will follow being born upon certain days, that many a mother has been known to make herself seriously unwell because her child has not been born on the day she wished it to be. The forecasts of the birthdays, which, like so many other examples of Warwickshire folk-lore, are done into rhyme, are believed in by the rustics with a strength which is as picturesque as it is sometimes fatal; for the knowledge of being born upon a "bad luck day" has a deteriorating influence upon the mind, and makes those so born careless, improvident, and neglectful of the future.

According to the rhyming forecast prevalent in Shakespeare's greenwood,

> Sunday's child is full of grace;
> Monday's child is fair of face;
> Tuesday's child is full of woe;
> Wednesday's child has far to go;
> Thursday's child's inclined to thieving;
> Friday's child is free in giving;
> Saturday's child works hard for its living;

and it is almost needless to say which three days of the week the Warwickshire rural mothers desire as the natal days of their offspring.

As there are forecasts in connection with the birthdays of children, so there are beliefs entertained and formalities observed in the country cottages of this neighbourhood whenever a member of the household dies. With the occurrence of death in the homestead it is the common practice to unfasten the lock of every door and to open all the doors of the house. There is a touch of the beautiful in this observance, for the idea is that nothing should be done to prevent the departed spirit from leaving its earthly habitation and soaring away to the heavenly mansions. All, therefore, is made clear for the passing of the spirit on its upward way. Wedded to this formality is the belief that when any one in the house dies the clock will stop at the moment of death.

Though some are sad and some are merry, there are beliefs in the indoor folk-lore of Shakespeare's greenwood which are not without a certain kind of humour. They are in the nature of shafts of ridicule, and are aimed, as a general rule, at women and their endeavour to show themselves the superior sex, though traditions may have dubbed them the weaker. In the country cottages of leafy Warwickshire it must be confessed that many of the housewives, according to their own showing, " wear the breeches " as the saying is among them ; and it is, perhaps, on this account that sundry, but singularly effective rhymes, having relations to the positions of the sexes, are in extensive use in the neighbourhood.

One certain sign of a man's conquest by a woman is, in the belief of these country folk, to be found in the condition of the herb sage, which grows in every cottage garden in this greenwood. If the sage dwindles and is leisurely in growing, then the husband has the laugh of the wife, because her triumph is not complete; but if it flourishes and shows signs of well-doing, then the goodman's power is gone, for the rhyme saith,

> *If the sage tree thrives and grows,*
> *The master's not master, and that he knows;*

and none, not even the person most concerned, ever doubts the truth of the words. The deposed master submits with becoming meekness, with the resignation of the fatalist that he generally is; and it is only when his wife whistles in exultation of her conquest that he will venture to retort with biting emphasis,

> *A whistling woman and a crowing hen*
> *Are neither good for gods nor men;*

a rhyme which may often be heard tripping in critical comment from the tongue of the Warwickshire rustic.

Such are some of the occurrences, formalities, practices, signs, and beliefs to which such strong adherence is paid by the dwellers in Shakespeare's greenwood. The lore of wood and water, tree and flower, bird and beast, wind and rain, life and death, is part of the character of these poetical, dreamy, far-seeing, and romantic country folk. Strip them of their lore and they would become ordinary and commonplace people. While they retain it, as they are likely to do for ages to come, they show themselves to be a quaint, picturesque race of humanity—worthy of the strength, individuality, and romance of their own woodland.

The Birds and Trees

The Bird's Sanctuary.—The Proud Tailor.—Leafy Leamington.—The Holly Walk : where Mr. Carker met Edith Granger.—The Town Rooks.—The Thieving Rook.—The Throstle.—The Missel-Thrush.—The Bullfinch.—The Bird-Catcher.—The Ring-Ousel.—The Landrail.—The Skylark.—The Companions of the Rustic.—The Skylark's Flight.—The Magpie as Seer and Socialist.—The Carrion Crow a Thief.—Jackdaws Building.—Rooks and Jackdaws at School.—An Entrance to the Forest of Arden.—The Prayer at Coughton Cross.—The Round Tree (the Middle of England).—Gospel Oaks.—The Pollard Oak at Stoneleigh Park.—Shakespeare's Oak in the Deer Park.—The Big Oak at Snitterfield.—"The Three Ladies."—Shakespeare's Crab-Tree at Bidford.—The Elms.—The Walnuts at George Eliot's "Hall Farm."—The Big Chestnut at Offchurch Bury, on the Site of Offa's (the Mercian King's) Palace.

The Birds and Trees

THOUGH the woodman with his axe has, during the past three centuries, made the once almost impenetrable Forest of Arden simply a set of woody remnants, there is still woodiness enough and leafiness enough in Shakespeare's greenwood to afford a pleasant sanctuary for Nature's minstrels—the birds. That was a glorious time for the feathered family when Warwickshire was so leafy and thickly wooded, that even in remembered times a squirrel might leap from tree to tree for the whole length of the county. But even now, when necessity has compelled landlords to turn some of their best-grown timber into necessary money, there are woods, and "dumbles" (little woods) and spinnies, studding both the Woodland and the Feldon, where any variety of bird can, as the Psalmist says, "lay her young."

Writing simply as a lover of birds and not as an ornithologist I am delighted to find that the greenwood which gave birth to the sweetest human poet that ever "warbled his native wood notes wild," also gives birth yearly to some of the sweetest poets in feathers that ever adorned and enlivened the haunts of Nature.

One of the prettiest of these is the goldfinch. This merry little gentleman, the fop of the finches, is called "the proud tailor" in Warwickshire on account of his fine dress and dainty carriage. He is becoming rarer in the greenwood near my home at Leamington every year owing to the incursions of the bird-catcher from Birmingham; who with lime, and net, and bag is continually in quest of him. The provisions of the Wild Birds' Protection Act do not seem of much value to the dandy little proud-tailor, who has to pay the full penalty for being beautiful—first by the loss of its eggs and the "lugging" of its nest, and next by the loss of its pretty self; being transported in the bird-catcher's green bag from the crab-tree in Shakespeare's woodland to an unknown place in a dull and smoky city.

The many "dumbles," or little woods in hollows, studded over the face of the landscape in this leafy shire make it a very pleasant country for the birds and for those who love them. Many of the towns, too, contain so much greenery that it is nothing unusual for some of the shyest of birds, and sometimes the rarest, to build their nests and rear their young in the gardens of villa residences in the busiest of thoroughfares. There are, perhaps, few towns where bird-life can be seen so prettily and so little under restraint as at Leamington, well named "the leafy." There is scarcely a street, terrace, circus, square, or road in this fashionable town where the high palatial dwellings are not adorned with trees whose luxuriant foliage affords an arbour in which the feathered families can build their house and rear their young.

In the very centre of the town, in that venerable Holly Walk which Dickens utilised in "Dombey and Son" as the scene where Mr. Carker first met Edith Granger, there is as fine a colony of rooks as a naturalist might only expect to find much farther from the madding crowd than the close proximity of tramcars, electric lights, and ever-bustling people. And the rooks have become acclimatised to the scene. Though it is but a ten minutes' walk from the Holly Walk Rookery (and, for a rook, only a three minutes' fly) to a landscape of field, wood, and water, the birds of this colony have outlived any shyness of which at any time they were possessed.

I have seen a rook fly out of the tree in which its nest was built down into the busy Parade for a piece of bread which it observed there, and dodge the cabs and trams and equestrians as cleverly as a lady would on a bicycle. In the middle of the day, too, when their young have grown big enough to see the world at a closer distance than from the top of an elm-tree, the old rooks will bring their families down to the gravel walk and strut about, with people on each side of them, with the most interesting unconcern—doubtless viewing the fashions of Vanity Fair with great delight.

From my observations of the doings of birds it has become clear to me that the law of the oppressor (the stronger against the weaker) is as rigidly honoured among the feathered as the human creation. One day two starlings, brilliant in new plumage, were lunching upon a crust lying in the roadway in front of my window. They were enjoying the repast excellently well, and I wondered at their unwisdom in not taking their "joint" nearer to a more secure place. Suddenly the birds uttered that peculiar rattle in the throat which starlings are accustomed to make when frightened, left off pecking the crust, and bent their heads down as if trying to escape some overhead calamity. A rook had been watching them from the chimney-stack of a neighbouring house, and in a shot swooped down upon the dainty morsel, and seizing it in its long beak, bore it away to its own rookery, leaving the starlings standing aghast at the creature's impudence.

At the east end of leafy Leamington, which is so sylvan that the thrush, "the throstle," as the rustic folks call it, may be heard singing in the morning and the nightingale at night in the Jephson Gardens, right in the middle of the town, there is a footpath leading through a landscape of mead, woodlet, and brook to the villages beyond, where the birds of Shakespeare's greenwood can be seen in all the glory of their natural life.

That engaging minstrel, the throstle, with speckled breast and flashing eye, is one of the first feathered folk to be met with in this one of the many enchanting scenes of pastoral Warwickshire. He is one of the residents of this greenwood, staying with us all through the year. In the early morning he will be seen on the topmost twig of one of the fir-trees that flank the western side of the Comyn Farm. His nest is probably in a fork of the bush beneath him, or in one of the stunted apple-trees growing in the orchard there. The song-thrush is one of the first birds to build in Shakespeare's greenwood. I have found its nest, well made and ready to receive the eggs, wedged in the knotty part of a hawthorn hedge before ever a single leaf has burst its bud, and with the nest exposed to the view of every eye.

Its handsome cousin, the missel-thrush, called in Warwickshire "the hoarse thrush," because it does not sing so sweetly as the song-thrush, is often seen dipping its yellow bill in a runnel, or standing erect in the pastures, previous to scudding off with a frightened note at the appearance of an intruder. This fine bird is a great ornament to these landscapes, and, when you can get a good look at him, will well repay the notice. But the missel-thrush is shy and reserved to human creatures, though at a distance, from a tuft of long grass, it will stand and survey them with a curious and interested eye.

The short musical pipings of the bold "bully," or bullfinch, are now heard with all the charm which a deep solitude gives to a scene beyond the haunts of men. There are two well-grown orchards hard by, one inclining towards the willow-fringed Leam, which Hawthorne in "Our Old Home" has called the laziest little river in the world, "lazier even than the Concord"; and where there are fruit trees with buds there will the bold finch be, performing his acrobatic exercises upon the extreme edge of a slender twig. Like his gayer and more exclusive relation, the goldfinch, the bullfinch is the object of the bird-catcher's assiduous care. His ruby breast, generally attractive appearance, and sweet little song, make him a favourite cage-bird, and he is accordingly much sought after.

In the greenwood near my home the bullfinch is not by any means so rare as the goldfinch; in fact, I have seen whole flocks of them round the Coomb Farm in the early summer; but that is scarcely a sufficient reason for the wholesale catching of this pretty and merry creature, whose only offence is that he has a fondness for tapping the buds of fruit trees. Doubtless the angry farmer who fires small shot at him does infinitely more damage to the tender buds than the bill of the bullfinch; and any harm "the bully" may do is, I think, amply atoned for by the number of insects he clears from the trees. I do not see the name of the bullfinch in the list of protected birds issued by the Warwickshire County Council, and that, I suppose, is why this well-known member of the finch family is made such fair game for the Birmingham bird-catcher; but if the catching is allowed to continue unchecked the gay bullfinch will soon be as rare in this greenwood as its relation, the goldfinch.

Owing to its solitary and woody character, many parts of Shakespeare's greenwood become the arbour of some extremely interesting and somewhat rare birds. One of these is the ring-ousel. This fine bird is similar in build to the blackbird, and is adorned with a beautiful white ring encircling the neck down towards the breast. So shy are these birds that it is very unusual for a bird-lover to get even a passing look at them.

They build their nests as a rule in the tangle of a ditch in very isolated places, far from the madding crowd. You may occasionally startle a sitting bird from its eggs (as I have done from a ditch on the north-east side of the Red House Farm at Lillington), with the result that a quivering motion will be seen to affect the blades of grass, as the ring-ousel skims through them with a "Cuck-cuck-cuck-oo-oo-oo" issuing from its throat in a softer key than the startling scream of its larger congener, the blackbird.

On the hill south of the ditch in which I have found the ring-ousel's nest more than one year, and where, I fancy, it builds every summer, there is usually a good crop of oats, and from there comes all day long the plaintive cry of the landrail. This bird is called a "corncrake" in Warwickshire, and its rail is sometimes heard in the fields unusually early. I have heard its cry from the bottom of the green wheat when the blades have been scarcely a foot high. Few birds are so reserved as the landrail. It shuns publicity, and only upon rare occasions can it be even seen, though by its mournful note it is known to be close at hand.

One day when quietly angling in the brook which winds round the western side of Offchurch Bury (the seat of the Earls of Aylesford), and near to the well-known woodlet, "The Rung Hills," where the stock of fur and feather is sufficient to delight the heart of the most exacting naturalist, a landrail whose crake had all morning long enlivened the silent air walked right out from the bottom of the green wheat on to the brook's bank; when, seeing me, it immediately turned tail and dived into the wheat again with a more agitated note. It is thus very difficult to get a good look at this landrailing bird, and being extremely fleet of foot it can cover a considerable space of ground in no time if it thinks it is being pursued. The young landrails present a rather unwieldy appearance, with their long necks and waddling gait.

This well-known denizen of Shakespeare's greenwood is one of the few birds who can fitly be called the companions of the rustic. The labourer who is hoeing the rising corn, or the woman who is gathering couch-weed or charlock, have always the landrail to keep them company, and if its note has not much joy in it (being, indeed, rather the reverse of cheerful) there is always the joyful and melodious song of the lark to cheer them on their way up and down the furrows.

The lark family (the skylark, woodlark, and titlark) are all plentiful in leafy Warwickshire; but the skylark with speckled breast and ravishing song is the favourite of them all. Himself a strong singer, Shakespeare had evidently a strong affection for the song-lark, as he speaks of this bird so many times. In that beautiful lyric in "Cymbeline" (Act ii. scene 3), beginning

Hark! hark! the lark at heaven's gate sings,

the poet shows clearly the rapture with which he had watched in his own greenwood the marvellous aerial flight of this poet in feathers. In Warwickshire the first bird to rise is the lark. When other dwellers in the greenwood are hanging like so many fluffy balls upon the twigs, the skylark is enskied over the ploughman's head, singing his matin-song to the sun, and putting the peasant in good heart for his day's labour.

Apart from its great gift of song, for which it is chiefly noted, the skylark has a wonderful strength of pinion. With dauntless courage the merry little fellow will mount through the most tempestuous wind if only the morning be bright. I have watched him in this greenwood being beaten down again and again by the force of the tempest, and scattered in a wide sweep from the place of his first ascent, only to rise again a minute or two afterwards and battle with the gusts until he reaches such an altitude as to look no larger than a gnat to the eyes of the watcher below.

Another constant companion of the field-worker in Shakespeare's greenwood is the loquacious lapwing. No field of turnips or green grain is complete in Warwickshire without the presence of this broad-winged, lapping-flighted bird, whose ceaseless cry of " Pee-wit, pee-wit " is a certain sort of company to the peasant in isolated quarters.

Lapwings have a heavy, swooping flight, and when a flock of them is seen wheeling low over the ground, with their white under bodies and black-tipped wings, they present a curious and interesting picture. They have, too, a peculiar downward-darting movement, as if they were about to attack the lonely peasant who may happen to be cutting thistles in the neighbourhood of their nest. In some of the sequestered pastures in these manless landscapes, I know of nothing more strange and weird than the sudden cry of "Pee-wit, pee-wit," as the bird laps from her nest, wheels upward round your head in ever-widening circles, and finally darts down again in anxiety for the well-being of her eggs and young, leaving the scene once more in silence.

That famous augur, the magpie, in beautiful plumage and lively spirits, is frequently to be seen on a summer's day among the fleecy flocks lying in the long meadow northeast of the Red House Farm, in search of insects. The sheep by long habit have come to know the magpie, and perhaps to appreciate him for his kind office in relieving them of divers flies that batten upon and torment them; for they seldom rise, though the bird busies himself about their fleece and chatters with no effort at restraint. The bird is a seer, as observed in another section of this volume, to the rustics of Shakespeare's greenwood. This is doubtless because magpies are so rarely seen in groups. One magpie which, in the superstitious calendar of the rustic, means sorrow to those who see it, is naturally seen oftener than three, which is supposed to denote a wedding ; hence the forebodings of these country folk in regard to the seeing of these lively birds.

The magpie is by no means so unsociable as some of the feathered denizens of this woodland. He seems, indeed, rather fond of company—if there is anything to be obtained thereby. One day I saw a group of small birds, consisting of tree and hedge sparrows, yellow buntings, and piefinches, rejoicing over the discovery of a small piece of meat they had found in a paddock near a thatched barn. The meat was too cumbersome for any of the small folk to fly away with, and so they hopped round it, and each one had a peck—seemingly in its turn.

In a few minutes a young magpie came hopping down out of a tree in which its nest was built, and, like an invited guest, took its place among the smaller birds ; having, with the rest, its peck at the piece of meat, and chattering to the birds beside him—telling them, doubtless, how much obliged he was for their courtesy. The picture of this single magpie sitting in that circle of birds, the biggest of which (apart from itself) was the yellow-hammer, may be readily imagined, and convinces me that the magpie must not be considered as an unsociable member of the feathered folk.

If the magpie is a bit of a thief—and I am afraid the charge is only too well founded—he himself is often made the victim of the predatory carrion-crow. This can be seen to advantage in building time, ere the elms and oaks of Shakespeare's greenwood are in full leaf.

Should you chance to see a pair of magpies making their nest in the, as yet, bare forks of the wych-elm, you will speedily observe a pair of carrion-crows settle in the same tree and hop down to the platform of twigs. The magpies may protest, but, in the knowledge of greater strength and power, the crows make light of the protest. A few flaps of the wings, a sharp dig or two with the sword-like beak, and the crows are masters of the situation. One by one they lift the twigs and bear them away for use in their own nest, and the poor magpies, sitting in silence and melancholy, behold their labours come to naught. It is strange that this indolent, cuckoo-like characteristic (this gathering of another's labour, so observable in the human race) should animate the fowls of the air, when there is so much material lying about for any and every bird to gather!

Something of the raven's weirdness seems to exist in the crow, the rook, and the jackdaw. One might call the carrion-crows lazy who rob the magpies of the sticks with which they have built their nests. In reality they are not idle, but full of a spiteful roguery; for it is a sober fact that crows will carry twigs which they have stolen from the nests of other birds for a considerable distance, when twigs equally as good and useful are lying immediately beneath their home.

One spring-time I was highly amused by the operations of a pair of jackdaws who had fixed their place for nesting in the steeple of a church. The edifice is situated quite on the skirts of the greenwood, and the daws need have gone no farther afield than down to the ground to have obtained all the material they required for their nests. Instead of which I saw them fly clean out of sight into the eastern woodland and come back after a considerable lapse of time, jadedly and heavily ploughing through the air, each with a good-sized twig in its beak! They had doubtless been fetching their sticks from some place well known to them far in the heart of Shakespeare's greenwood,

Under the shade of melancholy boughs.

There is no better place than the green pastures of Warwickshire in which to see the rooks and jackdaws "at school." In many of the "basins" to be found over the face of this charming county I have surprised these familiar birds seated in circles with two or three in the centre performing the parts of schoolmaster and teachers, and can say that nothing more like the real school has ever come under my cognisance in this famous of woodlands.

Near the south-western border of the county there is a well-wooded piece of park-land known as Coughton Park, the ancient estate of Sir George Throckmorton, who built the historical Coughton Court (where the Gunpowder Plotters made their rendezvous) in the reign of Henry the Eighth. At the southwest angle of the Park stands the base of an antique cross, now preserved by a ring of palings. This point is noteworthy from the fact that several centuries ago it was one of the entrances to the then great Forest of Arden.

Shakespeare's greenwood was then so thickly wooded that travellers, having to pass through the Forest on their way to adjoining counties, were in the habit of halting at Coughton Cross to pray for protection and deliverance from the robbers who were known to haunt the Forest in large numbers. This fact, added to the statement of Elton that even in modern times a squirrel might leap from tree to tree for nearly the whole length of the county, will serve to show that the terms "leafy" and "woody" are well applied when speaking or treating of Warwickshire.

Though the elements of Nature and the axe of man have for upwards of five hundred years made inroads upon the primeval fastnesses of the once great and almost impenetrable woodland, among the sered and wasting remnants of the Forest of Arden there are still left, in many parts of the park-land of the county, such monarchal trees as any greenwood might wish to boast.

By reason, not only of its historical and poetical fame, but also because of the fact of its being the central county of "Merrie England," the position of leafy Warwickshire ("the heart of England," as Drayton calls it) is marked at many points by the presence of trees to which great interest attaches. One of these is the celebrated "Round Tree," growing on the wayside between Leamington and the village of Lillington, and known far and wide as marking the site of the middle of England as correctly as the condition of measurements will allow.

The tree is a huge oak about thirty feet in girth, standing upon a green mound several feet from the ground, and is encircled by a fence of tall iron palings. It is thought to be a tree of great age, for in the days of the Civil Wars, the distressful Stuart days, when the soldiery of Oliver Cromwell passed through Lillington and Leamington (the latter at that time an isolated little hamlet of less than thirty homesteads all thatched with straw), on his way to meet the Royalists at Edge Hill, it was known and spoken of in the prints of the time as the Centre of England tree—a distinctive title which it holds to this day.

Even then it was a well-grown tree with a record of more than one century, and it is probable that the " Round Tree " is one of the few remaining large trees of the old Bins Wood, which formerly extended over a wide expanse of country in this neighbourhood (a portion of which is still known by the name of Binswood) and formed a small part of the great Forest of Arden. As it now appears, it is a strong, vigorous, and branching tree, graceful in shape, and beautiful in its summer leafage. It is a favourite subject for the painter and photographer, and pictures of it are to be met with in at least two continents —Europe and America.

Of oaks there are a goodly number in Shakespeare's greenwood, grown to a stately size, which attract attention, not only by their personal appearance and weight of years, but by the interesting associations which surround them. Leafy Warwickshire is, indeed, a county of Gospel Oaks, and many of these, like the others, are huge in growth and venerable in years. They formed the boundary lines or marks between adjoining parishes, and when the bounds were beaten the parson was wont to deliver his homily beneath the shady boughs. From this circumstance the trees have taken the name of "Gospel Oaks," and though Time has somewhat thinned their number, there are many still existing, dotted about in various parts of this sequestered greenwood.

Perhaps the largest, or one of the largest, of these Gospel Oaks, is that standing near Inchford Brook, on the boundary of the parishes of Warwick and Beausale. It measures twenty-seven feet in girth at a height of one yard from the ground, and is a typical example of the beauty of Warwickshire trees. The poet Herrick alludes to the custom of reading the gospel of the day under these oaks, at the annual perambulation of the parish boundaries, in the lines addressed to Anthea in "Hesperides":

*Dearest, bury me
Under the Holy-Oak or Gospel tree,
Where (though thou seest not) thou mayst think upon
Me, when thou yearly goest Procession.*

At a distance of five miles from the famous "Round Tree" at Lillington stands the spacious and historical Stoneleigh Park, the estate of Lord Leigh. Here the fine, and even majestic, trees of Shakespeare's greenwood are seen in all the fulness and beauty of their natural growth. The two divisions of the estate, the Deer Park and the Home Park, abound in magnificent specimens of oak, elm, ash, and beech, and beneath their spreading branches roam at will the fine herds of red and fallow deer, and the big-horned bullocks for which Stoneleigh is noted.

Of the numerous examples of well-grown timber which arrest the gaze at every turn in these beautiful Parks, there is an ancient pollard oak, standing in the Home Park near the Abbey, which demands more than usual attention. Shorn of its once proud top, its gigantic boughs have spread out downward, some of them approaching the ground, and now form a vast dome of greenery—a shelter from the rain and a screen from the sun. The tree, at a short distance from its base, is thirty-six feet in girth, the bark is well stretched out and of a soft green hue ; and standing there like a feudal sentinel of the ancient Forest, a guard of the stone walls of the romantic Abbey, this huge oak has a grandeur and a presence worthy of the historic woodland in which it grows, and in which Shakespeare is said to have often wandered.

The poet's steps, however, according to the traditions of the neighbourhood, were directed more frequently to the Deer Park than the Home Park. There the solitude would be deeper, the scenery wilder and more picturesque, the trees more varied and luxuriant, and, above all, there would be the herds of deer for him to watch, like his own Melancholy Jaques, from his place of retirement— beneath the boughs of a great oak near the present Rifle Butts, where, it is said (whether fiction or not cannot be determined), he lay along the green turf and composed some of his plays.

Had Shakespeare required only beautiful

scenery and colossal trees, he need not have gone so far to gain them as the famous Deer Park at Stoneleigh. They were to be had almost at his own door. The village of Snitterfield is but four miles from Stratford-on-Avon, and in the Park there is extant to-day an oak-tree which has probably the distinction of being the biggest in the whole of the Warwickshire greenwood. It is no less than forty feet ten inches in girth at the base, and at a height of six feet from the ground measures twenty-four feet six inches —a truly monarchal tree for an English landscape.

Not far from this giant representative of the ancient oaks of the primæval Forest of Arden there is another tree of goodly size which is a worthy companion to it. This tree is noteworthy from the fact of its being an ash, and having attained the somewhat unusual growth of thirty-five feet six inches in girth at its base. There is, indeed, a wealth of well-grown timber in the neighbourhood of Snitterfield ; the Park containing an avenue of fine elms, and the village itself being set amid such handsome specimens of woodland growth as would be difficult to surpass even in Shakespeare's greenwood, rich as it is in the products of ancient forestry.

The vicarage grounds and the churchyard of this historical village (of which Richard Jago, the Poet of "Edge Hill," and lifelong friend of Shenstone, was Vicar for twenty years) also contribute interesting trees to the number extant in leafy Warwickshire. On the well-trimmed lawn of this picturesque old gabled building there is a group of three remarkably graceful silver birch-trees, noteworthy not only on account of their size, but owing to the fact that they were planted by the poet Jago's daughter, and are known as "The Three Ladies." The churchyard contains a fine double yew and three unusually large lime-trees, supposed to be the biggest in the country, the finest of them measuring seventeen feet nineteen inches in girth at the base.

Shakespeare's greenwood (that portion of it which lies between Stratford-on-Avon and Bidford, passing through "The Haunted Hillborough" of the epigram) is as renowned for the crab-tree now as it was in the days when the poet conceived the character of Caliban, who knew where crabs grew. Along the shady lanes, for about six miles from Stratford towards Bidford, the hedgerows are frequently studded with crab and perry pear-trees ; and at a point in the roadway, less than a mile from Bidford (standing in a field on the left side), there is a young crab-tree which has a poetical and historical tradition attaching to it.

This young crab-tree is held by some to be the representative of the older one beneath whose boughs Shakespeare slumbered away the effects of the carouse he had upon a memorable occasion with the Bidford Society of Sippers. Others say that the historical tree (which has long since disappeared) under which the poet prostrated himself stood nearer the centre of the field than the site upon which the existing crab-tree now rears its youthful top. Which hypothesis is correct it would be difficult to determine ; but there seems to be no doubt that the field is the actual one in which Shakespeare was found ; and so the present crab-tree, rightly or wrongly, enjoys the proud distinction of being linked to a great name.

Though leafy Warwickshire contains more elm-trees than any other variety of tree, it is a curious fact that, in point of size, the elm will not compare favourably with the oak. There are few big elms in Shakespeare's greenwood. They are, as a rule, fine, straight, stately trees, and the ranks upon ranks growing out of the hedgerows in every field and lane appeal to the lover of Nature as one of the most charming features of a classic landscape ; but they do not grow to a colossal size—probably because the landowners find them so useful and valuable for the timber market. Their evenness of girth and height, and their prodigious number form such a feature of this county that Warwickshire might aptly be called " The Land of the Elms."

In the heart of the hardy north of the county, the very core, so to speak, of the ancient Forest of Arden, the walnut-tree used to be a feature of the woodland scene. The walnut, however, is now seen only at rare intervals. There are several fine ones to be met with in the immediate neighbourhood of Snitterfield and at Corley Hall (right in " George Eliot's " country), which is understood to be " The Hall Farm " of " Adam Bede "; but they are now graceful exceptions, well met with and justly admired, rather than familiar figures in the landscapes of Shakespeare's greenwood.

Unlike the rare walnut, the spreading chestnut-tree has a very large and popular representation in this leafy county. The chestnuts, indeed, are to be seen in all places—in park, field, lane, and hedgerow. One remarkable specimen has for centuries stood in front of Offchurch Bury, the present seat of the Dowager Countess of Aylesford, and the ancient site of the Palace of Offa, the Mercian king. The branches droop like a banyan-tree, and it is stated that as many as three hundred people have, at one time, stood beneath its boughs.

Such are some of the legacies left of the grand old Forest of Arden. Nearly every variety of tree is represented; and though civilisation has demanded that the axe of the woodman should be vigorously wielded, the charm of the Forest still lingers in leafy Warwickshire—the monarchs of the greenwood still wave their hoary arms in the sky space.

The Parson

The Festival on the Green.—At the Christening of the Great Bell, "St. Paul."—The Country Parson (Dr. Samuel Parr, LL.D.).—The Small Vanities of the Rustics, and the Parson's.—The Peal of Bells.—A Letter to a Norwich Friend.—A Lover of Dancing.—The Bowling Green at Leamington.—The Parson and the Duchess of Bedford in the Country Dance.—The Parson as Campanologist.—As a Student of Theocritus, Virgil, and Warwickshire Pastoral Life.—As an Amateur Gardener.—As a Friend of Landor's.—As Landor's Eulogist.—As a Merry-maker at the Easter Lifting.

The Parson

ONE bright summer morning, in one of the last years' of the last century, the green of the Parsonage-grounds in the sequestered village of Hatton, near the Elizabethan town of Warwick, in the heart of " Merrie England," was covered with a motley crew of people—the villagers of Hatton and the neighbourhood. A huge, brazen bell, looking like a miniature model of the celebrated Porridge Pot of the Giant Guy, then ensconced in the porter's lodge of the ancient Castle at Warwick, lay upon the green, the object of the interest and admiration of the assembled villagers.

It was a great day for the peasant, for the peasant's wife and daughter, and for the small growths of peasantry shooting up like the beets and horseradish in the kitchen-garden of the Parsonage.

It was, in fact, a high day; a festival. The good parson of Hatton was, above all things, a man, though as sound and orthodox a preacher as ever inveighed against the crafts and subtleties of the devil; and there was nothing the amiable Dr. Samuel Parr loved better than to gather round him the poorer members of his flock and to entertain them in the good old-fashioned style now gone out of date.

So there was a general holiday kind of appearance about the villagers; a brighter pair of tie-ups on William's breeches; a more showy waistcoat on young Ben; a dandy hat, slightly aside, on the well-nigh bald pate of Grandfather James; a spotless cotton bonnet on Dame Marjory's silver hair; a bunch of blue ribbons, bought at the last Warwick fair, peeping from beneath the large sun-hat of pretty, pert Harriet ; a new large curl on the brow of Johnnie's face ; a bright, pink sash round the pinafore of little Nancy ; and so on.

All these small signs of incipient vanity caught the eye of the jovial parson and did not displease him. In truth he liked them. He was not, he told himself, free from a touch of vanity in his own composition.

When he went down to Leamington Priors, then a tiny village all cornfields and pasturage, with less than thirty houses, all thatched with straw and built of dab and wattle, to lead off the country dance with the belle of the village on the Bowling Green, his heart often smote him for so easily giving way to his leanings towards the smaller vanities of the world ; and he frequently flushed at the thought of how particular he had been with his shoe-buckles, with his breeches-straps, and the tying of his neckcloth ; and how strictly he had enjoined the Warwick barber, who came to shave him, to give no quarter to the rising ranks, but to mow them cleanly off and leave not one hair behind.

Feeling that he himself was unregenerate, he could not be censorious to his villagers for the little fineries and trumperies displayed when they visited him at the Parsonage, especially when he knew that the brass gewgaw and the blue ribbons were decorations hung out upon the person in his honour, and for his particular admiration. So he observed them out of the corners of his eyes while not appearing to do so, privately rejoiced at the "dressy" tastes of his little flock, and inwardly reproached himself for his own worldliness.

And yet Dr. Samuel Parr was emphatically a good Christian. At the date of the Festival of the Bell he had been for many years Curate-in-Charge of the quaint little parish of Hatton, and during the whole of that time it is not recorded that he ever came in conflict with any member of his flock.

There do not seem to have been any upsets with the churchwardens in respect of altar ornaments; no conflict with the choir over the too loud notes of the bass-viol and hautboy; no wrangling with the richer members of the congregation in regard to the Latinised character of the sermons; no bother with the poorer parishioners on account of the dearth of eleemosynary doles ; no strivings with the farmers and occupiers of land over the tythes.

Everything had gone smoothly, for Dr. Parr was a man of peace, who loved his neighbour as himself, and delighted in their love perhaps more than he delighted in trimming his Parsonage-garden or writing classic poetry, for he was a great scholar.

It was his aim to be happy, and he was never so happy as when administering happiness to others. As he stood on the green, therefore, in three-cornered hat and well-powdered periwig, with his black surtout, white neckcloth, black stockings, low shoes, and silver buckles, looking very much like the portrait of his prototype, Dr. Samuel Johnson, who died the year before his birth, his broad face beamed with satisfaction at the simple, though true pleasures, observable among the rustics whichever way he turned.

Though so great a student of old-fashioned courtliness that his manner bordered upon the quaint, Dr. Parr, it would seem, was not superstitious ; for he christened his great bell on a Friday. And, strange to relate, no one there was troubled with forebodings of ill-luck. To make use of a somewhat trite phrase, though eminently applicable to the occasion, "all went merry as a marriage-bell."

The feelings of Dr. Parr upon the subject of the festival were those of an amiable enthusiast in campanology. This great bell on the green, and the others in the base of the church tower, making up the peal, were a great joy to him, and he was in ecstasy for his village friends to share in the joy. Those now much derided days were still "the good old days," for then the hand and heart went together—full, true, and open; and the well-to-do and the poor met in unrepressed fellowship in the grounds, and at the bidding of the former.

No waiting at the gate of Hatton Parsonage. No effusive greeting to the owner of a neighbouring manor, and a sidelong glance for the tenant of a thatched cottage; but the gate thrown open wide for all to enter, and a nod and beck, and wreathed smile for all alike—rich and poor.

Some idea of the enjoyment of parson and parishioners that day upon the green of the Parsonage-garden at Hatton may be gathered from the following letter sent by Dr. Parr to a Norwich friend a few days afterwards; an insight into the character of the man may also be gained thereby:

"My peal of bells is come. It cost a great deal of money, and I take the liberty of requesting you to forward the contribution which you promised me. I believe that my Norwich friends would have honoured me as a country parson if they had seen the harmless but animated festivity of my village on Friday last. The great bell has inscribed upon it the name of 'Paul,' and is now lying upon our green. It holds more than seventy-three gallons. It was filled with good ale, and was emptied too, on Friday last. More than 300 of my parishioners, young and old, rich and poor, assembled, and their joy was beyond description. I gave some rum to the farmers' wives, and some Vidonia and elder-wine to their daughters; and the lads and the lasses had a merry dance in the school-room.

"Now as the Apostle Paul preached a famous sermon at Athens, I thought it right that his namesake should also preach at

Hatton, and the sermon was divided under the following heads : ' May it be late before the great bell tolls for a funeral knell, even for the oldest person here present ! ' ' May the whole peal ring often and merrily for the unmarried ! ' ' May the lads make haste to get wives, and the lasses to get husbands, and hear the marriage-bell ! ' "

It will be noticed that in the above letter,

" *Great Parr, the Nestor of his age,*"

as Walter Savage Landor called him, speaks of a " merry dance."

Dr. Parr was not a religious curmudgeon. Though a divine of irreproachable earnestness, he had no faith in religion of a nature which would divorce every form of recreation from human life ; and in his day it was thought no sin for good Christians to enjoy, in moderation, the pleasures of the world, as in like manner they had to endure the world's pains. So the worthy parson of Hatton frequently held " a merry dance " in the school-room, and warmed his honest heart at the glow of spirits rising in the lissom frames of his bonnie lads and lasses.

In his own person dancing divided honours of delight with such performances as bell-ringing, gardening, and the writing of Greek and Latin poetry. He certainly owed nothing to his dancing-master. Proficient in that art as in divers others, he derived particular pleasure in practising it, and in observing the practice in others; and nothing but an attack of the gout or some other internal disquietude would prevent him from joining in "the merry dance."

When Dr. Parr was at the zenith of his popularity at Hatton in the early years of the present century, a new spring of saline water was found at Leamington Priors by the shoemaker poet of the village, and this, becoming known, attracted people thither, and paved the way for those frequent visits in which the country parson took particular delight. At the saline spring there in 1808 Dr. Parr made the acquaintance of young William Charles Macready, who subsequently became the greatest actor of his time; but what pleased him most, and coincided with his liberal tastes, were the invitations he received from the beautiful Duchess of Bedford, who was then "taking the waters," to go down to Leamington and join in the festivities of the village.

Her Grace had doubtless been made aware of the genial good-fellowship of Dr. Parr, as she already knew of his great talents in divinity and classical learning; for at this time, owing to his personal friendship with Charles James Fox, Edmund Burke, and Lord North, to whom he inscribed his edition of Bellenden's works, Dr. Parr had a famous reputation; and she was therefore anxious to include in her social party so great a literary and political lion as he undoubtedly was.

The Bowling Green at Leamington, where Sarah Kemble, afterwards Mrs. Siddons, during her residence as maid at Guy's Cliffe, was wont to foot it merrily with the lads and lasses of the village, was, at that time, situated at the south-east end of the old church, abutting on to the ancient coach-road (now High Street) and within hailing distance of the venerable coaching hostel, "The Black Dog," on the opposite corner.

There the cocking matches took place, the grinning through horse-collars, the sprunting, the horse-leaping, the morris dancing, and the

performances of the itinerant mountebank ;
there also the beau met the belle, and the
Tom Jones of the period tripped a measure
with the charming Sophia.

At certain periods, however, the Green
assumed a less riotous appearance, and was
used as the theatre for the representation of
those more harmless and picturesque customs,
such as the maypole dance, the performance
of rustic duologues, the country dance, and
other similar scenes of pleasantry associated
with life in a sequestered village at the end
of the last century and the beginning of
this.

Though as a learned Greek and Latin
scholar Dr. Parr stands out head and shoulders
higher than many cultured contemporaries, he
was, as I have said, by no means lacking in
those social, rural, humane, and domestic
qualities which give character and dignity to
manhood. He was as popularly esteemed in
the social as in the ecclesiastic, the literary,
and the political circle ; indeed, more so, for
he was one of those happily constituted men
who had not allowed his vast learning to
narrow down and starve the natural tastes for

consort with mankind which were an active force within him.

As a relief to his hard, laborious studies, therefore, this learned cleric of a country rectory, a dutiful and earnest worker and upholder of the Established Church, sought the lighter pleasures of life then to be found at Leamington Priors amid a select and well-informed company of visitors, attracted to the sylvan village by the fame of its saline waters.

There, it is recorded, that upon several occasions the scholarly and erudite divine from the charming little parsonage at Hatton took especial and particular delight in leading off the country dance on the Bowling Green with the beautiful Duchess of Bedford and other grand dames who were at that time resident in the village. In "The Rivals" Sheridan makes Falkland almost loathe the name of "country dance," because Bob Acres told him that his sweetheart, Julia, had danced in one; but such superlatively fine feelings do not seem to have had much influence with Dr. Parr. He danced often in them, and danced well—on the Bowling Green at Leamington and the green of his own village—and there is no doubt he greatly enjoyed the robust mirth of those fast disappearing country customs.

Nor was dancing the primary pleasure of this agreeable type of the old country parson. Dancing he loved, but he also loved bell-ringing and gardening, and all those rural occupations which are natural to the cultivated mind. Bell-ringing had been with him a growing taste from boyhood. It was even set down to his account as an eccentricity. While at school at Harrow, the contemporary of Lord Byron, and his neighbour Chandos Leigh, afterwards Baron Leigh of Stoneleigh, his fondness for campanology drew upon him undesirable attentions from his schoolfellows.

But a reputation for eccentricity did not disconcert Samuel Parr or lessen his interest in everything pertaining to bells. He weighed and rung the bells of Harrow with a courageous earnestness proof to every opposing influence, and no musician ever hung more lovingly upon a note than he upon the sonorous soundings of the church monitors.

This love of bells remained with him throughout his life. In his own village, as we have seen, he held a festival in honour of his great bell Paul, and here his enthusiasm was as natural as it was lively ; for during his tenure as curate in perpetuity at Hatton, a period of forty-two years, he cast or recast the whole of the six bells in the fine embattled fifteenth-century tower, and, as a respite from his parochial and classical labours, frequently rang a peal upon them. So ardent a campanologist was he, that he knew the tone and weight of every great bell in England at that time, and he was rarely so happy as when listening to the sweet tones of his own bells.

Apart from the terpsichorean and campanological arts, there were other pleasures in the life of a country parson admirably suited to the gentle inclinations of Dr. Parr. A continual study of the pastorals of Theocritus or the Georgics of Virgil had bent his tastes towards rustic pursuits, and upon divers occasions this venerable divine was seen among the cheery lads and lasses of his village in garments suitable to the scene, making hay in the meadows adjacent to the parsonage, watching the shepherd parting the lambs from the ewes or shearing the sheep ; or finally giving the dairymaid, as she sat milking the cows, a cheerful homily upon the blessings of content and good butter.

In his delight in rural pleasures and landscape-gardening Dr. Parr was, no doubt, greatly influenced by the works and careers of William Shenstone, the Poet of the Leasowes, a property on the borders of Warwickshire, and Richard Jago, the Poet of "Edge Hill," who was for twenty years Vicar of Snitterfield, a few miles from Hatton.

Shenstone, who wrote "The Schoolmistress," had long since gone to "that bourne from which no traveller returns," having died in 1763; and Jago followed his friend in May 1781, two years before Dr. Parr became curate of Hatton; but the sweet and peaceful nature of those two poets' lives so greatly fascinated the country-loving instincts of the Hatton parson, that immediately upon his preferment to the living he began to cultivate the Arcadian's art, and was daily seen with spade and rake in his little Parsonage-garden, trimming the plots and beds, and setting the plants and flowers that he loved.

Living in a purely rural and somewhat

isolated part of the country, Dr. Parr's opportunities for social intercourse with men of similar character and tastes to himself were necessarily rather limited; there was, however, at least one writer of genius with whom he maintained a lively friendship, and whom he frequently met, either in the cosy rooms of his own Parsonage or at his friend's residence under the historical East Gate at Warwick.

This was Walter Savage Landor, the Poet of the " Imaginary Conversations."

His quaint and often rugged manner, which was only the outside crust of a gentle, warm, and loving nature, was so akin to Landor's own, that the two poets became earnest and devoted friends; the elder giving the younger good counsel, and the younger brightening the years of the elder with the energy and ambition of a youthful and robust personality.

Dr. Parr, indeed, was affectionately attached to his young friend Landor. In introducing him to a literary acquaintance he wrote:

" He is impetuous, open-hearted, magnanimous, largely furnished with general knowledge, well versed in the best of classical writers, a man of original genius, as appears in his compositions, both in prose and verse; a keen hater of oppression and corruption, and a steady friend to civil and religious liberty. I am confident you will be much interested by his conversation, and it is my good fortune to know that his talents, attainments, and virtues amply atone for his singularities."

Even Landor, stern and unrelenting cynic as he was, could not have found fault with so kind and gentle a criticism. It was only one of the kindly actions that Dr. Parr took pleasure in performing, and the subject of his recommendation took special care to remember the friendship shown to him by the learned doctor.

One of the many merry customs observed in rural Warwickshire during the ministry of Dr. Parr was that maddest and merriest custom of "Easter lifting," and it was performed with unfailing regularity on the green at Hatton in the closing years of the last century and the opening years of the present.

The men lifted the women and kissed them on Easter Monday, and the women returned the compliment to the men on Easter Tuesday. It was a scene of the utmost mirth and liveliness, and one in which Dr. Parr, with his active sympathy with country pleasures, always took a warm interest; for his Whiggism was of that conservative type which delighted to sustain every custom which tended to strengthen the bond of sociality between the people.

Easter Monday, therefore, was a merry day at Dr. Parr's sequestered hamlet, but Easter Tuesday was the merrier. The jovial parson might fly from his ruby-lipped and bonnie-cheeked lasses who pursued him, with a view of adding additional sport to the ceremony; he might even hide himself in his great bell, Paul, in the belfrey of the tower, or offer to pay toll in lieu of being kissed. But this would not do for the lively and high-spirited maidens who had been lifted and kissed by him on the previous day. They would have no toll; nothing but the real thing; and so the willing country parson, like "laughter holding both his sides," must needs be led out to the green, lifted in the bonnie arms of the bouncing damsels, and kissed heartily by a dozen rosy lips.

This amiable and worthy representative of the old country parson, a type of rustic life which is now but a memory of an agreeable past, beloved by his villagers, and by all with whom he came in contact, laid down, not the burden of life, but rather its pleasures, on March 6, 1825, having ministered to the spiritual needs of Hatton for forty-two years.

A mural tablet in the church commemorates with simple candour the life and death of a man rich in all the finer feelings of human existence:

"*Great Parr, the Nestor of his age.*"

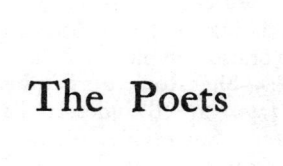

The Poets

Shenstone and the Leasowes.—At a Warwickshire School.—Meeting with Jago.—Jago's Apostrophe to Solihul.—Dr. Samuel Johnson nominated for Schoolmaster at Solihul School.—Shenstone at Pembroke College, Oxford.—With Jago at Beaudesert Parsonage.—Three Poets in Arden: Somerville, Shenstone, and Jago.—With Lady Luxborough at Barrells, Henley-in-Arden.—Shenstone's Lines to Lady Luxborough.—Her Ladyship's Poetry to Shenstone.—Her Letters and Death.—"Written at an Inn at Henley."—Death of Somerville (the Poet of "The Chase") at Edstone Hall.—Shenstone's Poetic Lament for his Friend.—Somerville's Epitaph.—Shenstone's Death at the Leasowes.—His Burial at Hales-Owen.—Jago's Poetic Lament for his Friend in his Poem of "Edge Hill."—The Fate of the Leasowes.

The Poets

ON the eastern borders of leafy Warwickshire, legally claimed as belonging to the county of Shropshire, though originally thirty miles distant from any part of that county, and delightfully hemmed in by the apple orchards of Worcestershire and the remnants of the ancient Forest of Arden in Warwickshire, lay the once charming and famous estate of the Leasowes, in the district of Hales-Owen.

There was born, on November 18, 1714, William Shenstone, whose name is inscribed on the Roll of Fame as "The Poet of the Leasowes."

Living so short a distance from the hallowed nook of Nature which gave birth to Shakespeare, it is not surprising that Shenstone should have formed so close an association with Warwickshire. A poet who could sing as he sung,

> For rural virtues and for native skies,
>   I bade Augusta's* venial sons farewell;
> Now 'mid the trees I see my smoke arise,
>   Now hear the fountains bubbling round my cell,

would be quite sure to find in the landscapes of Shakespeare's land the scenes of pastoral beauty which a gentle mind like his could so much admire. He did, indeed, as I shall presently show, find both scenes and friendships there which often brought joy to his tranquil and somewhat melancholy life.

Probably Shenstone's first connection with Warwickshire occurred in his boyhood, and the first haunt of those youthful and happy days was the Grammar School at Solihul, a

* London.

small town a few miles south of Birmingham, and at that date, and even now, a very charming semi-rural seat of learning.

I think it was owing to his early sojourn at Solihul as a pupil of the Rev. Mr. Crumpton, that caused Shenstone to become so attached to Warwickshire, for at the school there he formed that lifelong friendship with Richard Jago of Beaudesert, near Henley-in-Arden, which was so productive of enjoyment, and largely developed that turn for pastoral and descriptive poetry which in after life gave such a charm to his character.

Shenstone and Jago were supremely happy in each other's company, but I am afraid that their days, under the watchful and stern eye of the schoolmaster, were not so sweet and peaceful as Shenstone's were when at Hales-Owen in the Dame School of Sarah Lloyd, the lady whom he afterwards immortalised in "The Schoolmistress." It is clear, indeed, from the following lines of Jago, written at a subsequent date, that their actual life at school was not supremely pleasant :

*Hail Solihul! respectful I salute
Thy wall; more awful once! when from the seats
Of festive freedom and domestic ease,
With throbbing heart to the stern discipline
Of pedagogue morose I had returned.*

This Grammar School at Solihul was an ancient foundation dating from the reign of Richard the Second. Shenstone and Jago were two of the most famous celebrities which it nurtured; but it has also another important connection with English literature which will be interesting to allude to at this point.

In 1735, when twenty-six years of age, Dr. Samuel Johnson was nominated for the office of schoolmaster, and to have had such a literary celebrity in its midst would have added to the fame of Warwickshire; but the trustees of the Grammar School declined Johnson, because, as the Vicar of Solihul wrote to them, "he has the character of being a very haughty, ill-natured gent, and yet he has such a way of distorting his face (which though he cannot help) ye gentlemen think it may effect some young ladds."

So the author of "The Vanity of Human Wishes" was lost to Warwickshire.

From Solihul the embryo Poet of the Leasowes entered at Pembroke College, Oxford, where, it is said, he was chiefly remarkable for what was then counted the odd practice of wearing his own hair, which, being coarse in quality, little tended or dressed by its owner, and floating down over a large ungainly person, excited some ridicule, and constituted him one of the "characters" of his College. After four years of University life, Shenstone returned to the calmer joys of the Leasowes, to which property he had now succeeded, and began that course of poetic composition and landscape gardening which has rendered his name famous.

Thus commenced his close association with Warwickshire and his friend Jago, the subsequent Poet of "Edge Hill," a man whose spirit was so akin to his own that he enjoyed with him, until his death in February 1763, the most true and cordial fellowship. With Jago in the Forest of Arden—for the Parsonage of Beaudesert, where Jago was born in 1715, is right in the midst of the old Forest and adjacent to the ancient and quaint town of Henley-in-Arden, which at that time boasted of one of the finest Market Crosses of the fifteenth century then extant—the fire of poetry was kindled within him, and we hear him singing in "The Charms of Precedence" the praises of Shakespeare's classic river :

> *Where Avon rolls her winding stream,*
> *Avon! the Muses' favourite theme ;*
> *Avon! that fills the farmers' purses,*
> *And decks with flowers both farms and verses.*

It is no wonder that it should have been so. The Parsonage at Beaudesert is attached to the church of St. Nicholas, of which Jago's father was Rector, and both are placed at the foot of the Castle Hill, in a scene which would inspire poetry in the most unpoetic soul.

Eastward is the historic in-Arden town of Henley, and a little farther east the delightful seat of Barrells Hall, immured in park and woodland; northward are the now sered and wasting remnants of the old Forest surrounding Baddesley Clinton—"The Moated Grange" of Shakespeare; southward, towards the Feldon of Warwickshire, is the famous

Elizabethan town which gave birth to the greatest genius the world has ever seen ; and in the south-western corner stands the far-famed Edge Hill—a long elevated ridge on the northern slope of which the battle that has made its name famous in England's martial history was fought between the King's and Cromwell's soldiery on October 23, 1642.

Amid these and kindred scenes Shenstone and Jago took their happy way, making songs as they went. Up Edge Hill and into the Round Tower they doubtless often journeyed ; for it was the prospect, as seen from this famous elevation, that inspired those graceful reflections in Jago's mind which afterwards found expression in that fine descriptive poem " Edge Hill." By-and-by, too, the thoughts which these enchanted scenes created in the breasts of these two poets of Nature were to affiliate them to yet another poet and poetess, both living in the same poetic ground, and both inspired with feelings in harmony with their own.

A few miles south of Beaudesert—between there and the historic village of Snitterfield, where Jago was subsequently Vicar for twenty years, and where he died and was buried in May 1781—there stood, when Shenstone was visiting these Warwickshire haunts, a venerable mansion named Edstone Hall. There, in 1692, was born William Somerville, the descendant of a family which had owned the estate from the reign of Edward the Fourth. He became a skilful sportsman, a useful justice of the peace, and a somewhat brilliant poet and man of letters.

With Somerville the two friends, Shenstone and Jago, became on terms of affectionate intimacy, and often in the charming grounds of Edstone, overlooking the beautiful fox-gloved fringed Avon, where Somerville wrote his famous poem "The Chase," this poetic trinity enjoyed the conviviality which springs from the company of minds so well suited to each other as these were.

The poetess—for she had certainly tasted of the Pierian spring—who lent grace, charm, and learning to the brilliant literary coterie in the Forest of Arden was Henrietta, Lady Luxborough.

Her Ladyship was the only daughter of Henry, Viscount St. John, and half-sister to the celebrated Viscount Bolingbroke, Principal Secretary of State to Queen Anne, and the friend and executor of Pope. She was married in 1727 to Robert Knight, of Barrells Hall, Warwickshire—a mansion beautifully seated in the Woodland, a little way east of Henley-in-Arden, and within a very short distance of both Beaudesert and Edstone—who, in 1756, was created Lord Luxborough of Shannon, Ireland, and in 1763 (after Lady Luxborough's death), Earl of Catherlough and Viscount Barrells.

This marriage proved an unhappy one, and for the last few years of her life Lady Luxborough was separated from her husband, but continued to reside at Barrells Hall; where herself, Somerville, Jago, and Shenstone formed one of the most charming circles of poetic spirits which the literature of the last century afforded.

Shenstone was evidently much attached to Lady Luxborough and deeply in love with Barrells, which, considering its beautifully secluded situation, is not surprising. In the following lines he took occasion to pay a double compliment :

> *When first, Philander, first I came*
> *Where Avon rolls his winding stream,*
> *The nymphs how brisk, the swains how gay,*
> *To see Asteria, queen of May!**
> *The parsons round her praises sung!*
> *The steeples with her praises rung!*
> *I thought no sight that ere was seen*
> *Could match the sight of Barrells Green!*

There is also a suspicion that the lady's feelings towards Shenstone were those of sincere admiration for his poetic genius, if of nothing warmer. They both addressed each other in rhyme and prose; and if the poet was graceful, tender, and complimentary, Lady Luxborough was sweet, polite, and vivacious. Shenstone's feelings for the Lady of Barrells Green were very happily expressed in " An Irregular Ode," written after sickness in 1749, and which contains some very pure and tuneful poetry:

> *By flowery plain or woodland shades*
> *I fondly sought the charming maids;*
> *By woodland shades or flowery plain*
> *I sought them, faithless maids! in vain;*

* May festivals and morris dancing were customs greatly in vogue at Henley-in-Arden and Barrells in Shenstone's days.

*When, lo! in happier hour,
I leave behind my native mead
To range where Zeal and Friendship lead,
To visit Luxborough's honoured bower.*

Lady Luxborough herself had a pretty turn for poetry, and I think the lines which she addressed to Shenstone are a sincere compliment to the lovely picture which he made of the Leasowes:

*'Tis Nature here bids pleasing scenes arise,
And wisely gives Cynthia to revise;
To veil each blemish, brighten every grace,
Yet still preserve the lovely parent's face.
How well the Bard obeys each valley tells,
These lucid streams, gay meads, and lovely cells;
Where modest Art in silence lurks conceal'd
While Nature shines so gracefully reveal'd;
That she, triumphant, claims the total plan,
And with fresh pride adopts the work of man!*

Their friendship, indeed, was of that true and cordial character which gives lustre to human life, and it has certainly added a new charm to the literary history of Warwickshire, already so rich with the glories of many pens.

The letters of Lady Luxborough to Shenstone, written from Barrells Hall, are admirable examples of the epistolary art of the eighteenth century, and the poet himself paid a graceful tribute to the writer of them when he wrote with his own hand on the flyleaf of the cover in which they were bound the inscription: "Letters of the Right Honourable Lady Luxborough, written with abundant care, politeness, and vivacity; in which she was scarce equalled by any woman of her time. They commenced in the year 1739, and were continued to the year of her death, 1756, with some few intermissions."*

Shenstone was almost inconsolable at the death of Lady Luxborough; she had so greatly cheered his life and bound it up with the scenes in which she resided. But he had had one great friendship in Warwickshire broken before the passing away of the Lady of Barrells. This was his friend and brother poet, Somerville, with whom he had spent so many happy hours at Edstone Hall and in sauntering about the neighbourhood.

These two poets, who so closely resembled each other in talents, feelings, and habits, afford a touching picture of pure friendship

* This Correspondence was published in 1775.

too early riven by acts which might have been avoided. Though Shenstone was extravagant, and addicted to the coarser pleasures of life, as one may judge from those exquisite verses of his " Written at an Inn at Henley," the last of which,

> *Whoe'er has travelled life's dull round,*
> *Where'er his stages may have been,*
> *May sigh to think he still has found*
> *The warmest welcome at an Inn,*

will for ever be more closely associated with his name than any of his other poems, it is not recorded that he went to extremes. Somerville, on the other hand, is known to have done so, and his death, which took place in 1742 at Edstone Hall, was hastened by habits of intoxication, to which he gave way in consequence of the embarrassments resulting from his extravagance.

The Poet of "The Leasowes" bitterly mourned the sad end of his friend the Poet of "The Chase," and remarked indignantly on the grievance of a man of genius being asked to pay his debts: "For a man of spirit, conscious of having (in one production at least *) generally pleased the world, to be plagued and threatened by wretches that are low in every sense ; to be forced to drink himself into pains of the body, in order to get rid of the pains of the mind, is a misery." And then he laments him in a verse of touching sadness :

> *Near Avon's banks, on Arden's flowery plain,*
> *A tuneful shepherd charmed the listening wave;*
> *And sunny Cotsol' fondly loved the strain,*
> *But not a garland crowns the shepherd's grave!*

Somerville was interred in the exquisite little church at Wootten Wawen, one of the most interesting in all Warwickshire, and, after the death of his friend, undoubtedly one of Shenstone's most favourite and revered haunts. It is situated midway between Beaudesert and Edstone, is surrounded by woody landscapes, and was pronounced by Bishop Phillpotts, the late Bishop of Worcester, the most delightful church in the whole of his diocese.

In the lower portion of the Tower it contains the only undisputed Saxon remains in the county ; the Tower, being centrally

* "The Chase."

situated, has a Saxon chancel-arch which is supposed to be the narrowest in England. The church at Wootten Wawen is also famed for its chained books, of which there are so many that they may be said to almost form a library. Those of the greatest interest and value among them are the works of Bishop Andrews, Jewel's " Apology," and a Prayer-Book of the time of Charles the First.

The Lady Chapel contains the tomb of Somerville, and among others are monuments to the members of the Knight family of Barrells Hall. By Somerville's own direction his remains are covered simply with a plain stone; but even here Shenstone's friendship followed his departed brother-poet, for the inscription upon the stone is said to be from his hand. It is written in Latin and thus translated :

HERE LIES BURIED

WILLIAM SOMERVILLE, Gentleman,

WHO DIED 17 JULY, 1742.

If you discern anything good in me, imitate it. If you see a fault in me, avoid it with your utmost strength. Trust in Christ, for know that your life is uncertain, and death is sure.

After the death of his two friends, Lady Luxborough and Somerville, the visits of Shenstone to his beloved haunts in Warwickshire became much less frequent, and now that Jago had settled at the Rectory of Snitterfield, the journey was somewhat farther for him than "Luxborough's honoured bower" in the seclusion of Barrells; but though he had now sequestered himself more amid his own created charm at the Leasowes, his affection for the old pastoral haunts in the Forest of Arden were as sincere as ever, and he would be sometimes lured back to them from his native Eden.

This charming rural poet, whose association with Warwickshire entitles him to almost rank as the countryman of Shakespeare, Drayton, and Landor, having gone on a visit to Lord Stamford at Enville, caught cold on his return, and this being neglected, developed a fever, from the effects of which he died on February 11, 1763. He was buried by the side of his brother in the churchyard at Hales-Owen, and lies in the very heart of the beautiful spot now and for always identified with his name.

No one more sincerely mourned his loss than his faithful friend Jago, who, after a visit to his grave at the Leasowes, wrote the following lines to his memory in the poem of "Edge Hill":

> *Nor can the Muse while she these scenes surveys*
> *Forget her Shenstone in the youthful toil,*
> *Associate; whose bright dawn of genius oft*
> *Smoothed my incondite verse; whose friendly voice*
> *Called me from giddy sports to follow him*
> *Intent on better themes. . . . No more for me*
> *A charm it wears,* since he, alas! is gone*
> *Whose genius planned it, and whose spirit graced.*

If Shenstone's fame as landscape-gardener is greater than his fame as a poet, it must at least be owned that he has written some of the sweetest and most tuneful pastorals in English poetry. He was not a great poet, but he had the greatness within him which is born of a true love of Nature; and there is no doubt that his lifelong devotion to "Leafy Warwickshire" and its beautiful scenery inspired in his mind, as it did in Shakespeare's, many of the smoothest and prettiest lines which a true poet of country

---

* The Leasowes.

life has ever written. Yet, after all, as it has been well said, "The Leasowes" is the finest of Shenstone's poems, though it will not endure as long as any of his others ; its beauty, indeed, has long been shorn by new owners, to whom the poetry of a landscape is the merest figment.

The Novelist

The Way to "Cheverel Manor."—The Griff Miner's Ignorance of George Eliot and her Books.—South Farm: the Birthplace of the Novelist.—Arbury Hall. —A Romance in the Life of Charles Brandon, a former Owner.—Sir Roger Newdigate ("Sir Christopher Cheverel").—Robert Evans ("Adam Bede").—Gothicising the Hall.—Scenes of "Mr. Gilfil's Love Story." —The Death of Sir Roger Newdigate.—Griff: George Eliot's Native Village.—The First Railway in Shakespeare's Greenwood.— Mr. Newdigate's Canal.—To London by Water.—Chilvers Coten (the "Shepperton" of the Novelist).—The Original of "Mr. Gilfil."—The Village of Corley and the "Hall Farm" of Adam Bede. —George Eliot, the Novelist-Historian of Shakespeare's Greenwood.

The Novelist

IF a stranger were wandering down the narrow and leafy Warwickshire lanes between Bedworth and Nuneaton, and were to halt, say, in front of that well-looking house at Griff—the largest among the nine or ten that constitute the coal-bound parish—under the rooftree of which George Eliot formerly lived; if this stranger were to stop one of those dark-skinned men he might by chance meet there—though they spend most of their waking and working hours in the sunless streets of a coal mine—and ask him the way to "Cheverel Manor," the man would take his pipe from his mouth—for a collier *will* smoke in spite of all the legislators in the world—look hard at the stranger, shake his woolly head, and say, with a half-smile upon his face at the humour of a person having missed his road :

"Ney, you mun be cum the wrong road, I doubt. 'Appen you hev missed your way, sir. I hanna ever heered on a place wi' that name."

But if the stranger should improve upon the mistake by saying that he meant Arbury Hall, the miner's face would smile even through its duskiness, and he would be sure to say :

"Oh! you means old Charley's place. Poor old Charley Newdigate, him as died a many year ago—as good a gaffer, sir, as 'appen I shall ever drive a pick for, above ground or below ground either. Oh! yes, sir, I can show ye the way to Arbury Hall, an' I hanna gooin' to be long abouten it, I reckon. But as for Chev'ral Manner, or what you calls it, as ye spoke on, why I hanna ever heerd tell on that name i' these parts; an' I've lived i' Griff an' Beddorth, man an' boy, this forty year an' better."

By the same token that a man is no hero to his own valet, a mere writer of books is "a poor critter" in the eyes of Strephon, even when Strephon is covered with coal dust instead of the agricultural loam. A writer, born in the midst of squalid and rural surroundings, may often be monstrously clever in the art of making books, but to his neighbours, who know nothing of books except the Bible —and sometimes not much of that—he is a pitiful object indeed, and fair game for the wit that is indigenous to the bucolic and the mining mind.

Those whose armour has been pierced by a jagged shaft of humour shot from the broad mouth of a villager—be he miner, ploughman, cowman, or village mole-catcher—will know that sometimes this wit, by its very crudeness and rawness, wounds more deeply than the satiric arrows of a polished and cultivated mind.

And so George Eliot, "a monstrously clever woman," as a friend of mine, a former Bedworth coal-master, and a man who knew

Mary Ann Evans in the flesh some twenty years or more ago, is always fond of repeating, is no heroine to her own countrymen. Some of the more rough diamonds among them would look as confused at the name of George Eliot as at Cheverel Manor ; and the stranger who had the hardihood to ask for direction to " Shepperton Church " would be met with the reply that,

" Theer inna a church on that name i' these parts. Theer be Coten, Beddorth, Exhul, Astley, and Corley ; but I donna mind heerin' tell on such a place as Shep'ton. You mun mean Coten, I 'spect, or 'appen Beddorth, wheer Master Evans be parson."

Perhaps this, to the literary person, painful lack of knowledge or remembrance of a singularly gifted writer on the part of her own immediate country people, may be accounted for with two reasons : one, that many inhabitants of those little villages, clustering together in warm, loving groups, from which George Eliot drew most of her characters, have ceased to weave the warp and woof of life, being long ago laid to rest under the chestnuts in the quaint little graveyard; and, secondly, because the average villager is no more bookish now than in the days when "Adam Bede" found its way to Griff and clove an entrance into the hermetically sealed intellects there, and this simply owing to the fact that so many of them knew for certain that they were "put in" the book.

Extended education makes little headway in small towns and villages, and what there is is unfavourable to the maintenance of even recent tradition. The oldest inhabitant dies, perhaps, however, not before having performed the duty of handing down to his children and grandchildren the oral traditions of the place; but alas! his children and grandchildren " inna given to the writin' o' things down "—on paper or in their memory; and so as, one by one, the old inhabitants disappear, the oral traditions of the village disappear with them, until there is but one legend left of all that there might have been, and that so faintly remembered as to be almost a doubt.

But the cadaverous and painfully careful historian, a man from the bricked-in square of a colossal city who writes for the future, at a very small price per page, makes some amends for the forgetfulness of the oldest inhabitant. He writes everything down, prints everything he has written, places his book in a library where it is never, or hardly ever, opened, and then dies of a broken heart—accelerated by long years of wanton neglect and biting poverty.

Arbury Hall will, in the ages to come, be noted for its connection with George Eliot, who has made it " the Cheverel Manor " about which the Griff miner " hanna ever heerd on." In the far past, however, that lean and pale man, the writer of contemporary history, was busy there, and there is also a glamour of romance associated with a former owner of the Hall which has not found its way into George Eliot's books or even into the guide-books of the day ; but which is, nevertheless, a fact which greatly adds to the interest of this neighbourhood, in the midst of which the famous Sir Roger Newdigate raised his ecclesiastic and semi-Gothic pile.

A six-mile walk from the city of " Three Tall Spires," along the shady and pleasant road that leads to Nuneaton and on to Leicester, brings the traveller to Griff and Bedworth, and close to the "Cheverel Manor" of "Mr. Gilfil's Love Story."

That South Farm, too, where George Eliot was born on that dull November morning in 1819, will be within measurable distance of the traveller's survey. A very long time ago, before the Newdigates became the possessors of Arbury, there was in existence, near the Park, a farm known as Temple House. It was an old building surrounded by a moat, and belonged to the principals of an ancient manor thereabouts, called the Manor of St. John of Jerusalem.

Surely the South Farm in which Mr. Robert Evans used to reside, and in which his illustrious daughter first saw the light, must have risen from the ruins of Temple House.

Before it was ecclesiastic—which it became under the hand of Sir Roger Newdigate, the Gothic-loving baronet of "Cheverel Manor" —Arbury Hall was monastic. It was called "Erebury Priory," and was founded in the reign of Henry the Second, by Ralph de Sudely, as a house, or rather home, for the St. Augustine Order of Canons. At the Dissolution of Monasteries, in the twenty-sixth year of the reign of Henry the Eighth, Erebury Priory was suppressed, and its possessions granted by Royal Letters Patent to Charles Brandon, Duke of Suffolk.

It is at this point in the history of "Cheverel Manor" that the romance comes in which is not to be found in any of George Eliot's books, and does not appear in the topographical prints of the period.

A very rare pamphlet, of which it is supposed there are only two copies now extant, entitled "English Adventures," was printed and published in 1667. It dealt with strange occurrences which had befallen old and noble families of the time; and no doubt, as many of the adventures thus publicly promulgated were repugnant to the descendants of the families concerned, steps were taken to suppress as many of the pamphlets as possible.

One of the adventures was connected with the life of Charles Brandon, one of the early owners and occupiers of Arbury Hall, or

"Cheverel Manor," when in its monastic form, and was as follows:

"Upon the death of his lady, the father of Charles Brandon retired to an estate on the borders of Hampshire. His family consisted of two sons and a young girl, the daughter of a friend lately deceased, whom he had adopted as his own child. This lady, being singularly beautiful, as well as amiable in her manners, attracted the attention of both brothers. The elder, however, was the favourite, and he privately married her; which the younger, not knowing, and overhearing an appointment of the lovers the next night in her bed-chamber, he, thinking it a mere intrigue, contrived to get his brother otherwise employed, and made the signal of admission himself.

"His design, unfortunately, answered only too well. On a discovery the lady lost her reason and soon afterwards died. The two brothers fought and the elder fell — cut through the heart. The father broke down and went to his grave in a very short time. Charles Brandon, the younger brother, and the unintentional author of all this misery, quitted England in despair, with a fixed determination of never returning. Being abroad for several years, his nearest relations supposed him to be dead, and began to take the necessary steps for obtaining his estates. Aroused by this intelligence, he returned secretly to England, and for a time took private lodgings in the vicinity of his family mansion.

"While he was in this retreat, the young King, Henry the Eighth, who had just buried his father, was one day hunting on the borders of Hampshire when he heard the cries of a female in distress issuing from an adjoining wood. His gallantry immediately summoned him to the place—though he then happened to be detached from his courtiers—when he saw two ruffians attempting to violate the honour of a young lady.

"The King instantly drew his sword upon them, and a scuffle ensued which aroused the reverie of Charles Brandon, who was taking his morning walk in an adjacent thicket. He immediately ranged himself on the side of the King, whom he did not then know, and by his dexterity soon disarmed one of the ruffians, while the other fled.

"Charmed with this act of gallantry, so congenial to his own mind, the King inquired the name and family of the stranger, and not only repossessed him of his patrimonial estates, but took him under his own immediate protection.

"It was this same Charles Brandon who afterwards privately married King Henry's sister, Mary, Queen Dowager of France; which marriage the King not only forgave, but created him Duke of Suffolk, and continued his favours towards him to the last hour of the Duke's life. He died before Henry; and the latter showed in his attachment to this nobleman that, notwithstanding his fits of caprice, he was capable of a cordial and steady friendship.

"He was sitting in Council when the news of Suffolk's death reached him, and he publicly took occasion both to express his own sorrow and to celebrate the merits of the deceased. He declared that during the whole course of their acquaintance his brother-in-law had not made a single attempt to injure an adversary, and had never whispered a word to the disadvantage of any one; 'And are there *any of you*, my Lords, who can say as much?' The King looked round in all their faces, and saw that confusion which the consciousness of secret guilt naturally drew upon them."

From the fact related in the early history of Charles Brandon—who, upon being created Duke of Suffolk, and having the estates of Arbury granted to him by the King, went to live there—the poet, Thomas Otway, took the plot of his tragedy, " The Orphan." To avoid causing unnecessary pain, however, to descendants of the families affected who were living at that time, Otway transferred the scene of his tragedy from England to Bohemia.

The character of Antonio, which the dramatist would appear to have elaborated with great pains into an old debauched senator, raving about plots and political intrigues, is supposed to have been intended for that eminent personage, Anthony, the first Earl of Shaftesbury.

So late ago as 1825 there was a large painting of the Brandon incident at Woburn, and the old Dowager Duchess of Bedford, in showing this picture to a nobleman a few years before her death, is said to have related all the particulars of this romantic story.

Associations like these serve to make the site of the "Cheverel Manor" of George Eliot doubly interesting, and the marvel is that the author of "Scenes of Clerical Life" did not make use of this pretty romance in some way. But George Eliot was essentially a delineator of modern manners, not a writer of historical scenes—except in the case of "Romola"; and so the visitor to Arbury Hall must look elsewhere for the early history of the place.

It is a little curious, however, to find that an ex-Queen of France, and a noble Duke, used formerly to walk through the fine tree-studded Park where the late Charles N. Newdigate (strange contrast!) was wont to sit and frame his measures for keeping atheists out of the House of Commons; measures which, after his demise, no one, rightly or wrongly, thought it worth while to sustain.

The heirs of Charles Brandon, in the reign of Queen Elizabeth, sold Arbury Hall and the estates to Sir Edmund Anderson, Chief Justice of the Common Pleas. He, possibly out of respect for the stern Protestantism of his Royal Mistress, and with a desire to win her favour, demolished the old monkish house and built from the ruins what Dugdale calls a " fair structure of quadrangular form." No sooner was this building completed—in the twenty-eighth year of the reign of Queen Elizabeth—than the legal knight fostered a dislike to it, and passed the estate away in exchange to John Newdegate for the Manor of Harefield in Middlesex, where the Newdegate family had been seated since the days of Edward the Third. The Newdegates thus made Arbury Hall their family seat and began to spell their name with an *i*.

In 1734 the estates descended to Sir Roger Newdigate, who acquired the title from an ancestor. He seems to have been a gentleman of much note, attached very strongly to literature and the fine arts, and particularly devoted to the study of archæologian architecture. He, as George Eliot points out in " Mr. Gilfil's Love Story," had made " the grand tour " of European cities and returned, doubtless, deeply in love with the mansions of Italy, and rather ashamed of " the fair structure of quadrangular form " at Arbury, to which he had succeeded when only sixteen years old.

Sir Roger, indeed, would seem in many respects to have been endowed with exceptional abilities. He was born in 1718, presumably at Harefield, for in the very year of his majority he was elected Member of Parliament for Middlesex in the Tory interest. At Oxford, where he won the highest honours, and formed the most distinguished friendships, Sir Roger Newdigate secured enviable popularity.

After being the Parliamentary representative of Middlesex for six years, he was elected Member for the University of Oxford and held that position for thirty years. During that period he made "the grand tour" already spoken of, and in conjunction with Sir Horace Walpole, to whom he was much attached, worked energetically to revise the beauties of the Gothic style in architecture.

Scarcely a better building for the titled architect to try his hand upon could have been found than the Arbury Hall of that period. Some idea of the nature of the building may be gathered from a survey of the present stablings, which form a considerable portion of "the fair structure" erected by Sir Edmund Anderson. From each front of the house there were piles of projecting chimneys, and these, together with the unsightly chambers and bare brick walls, could not fail to offend the fastidiously cultivated eye of Sir Roger Newdigate—Italianised as it was by many years of foreign travel.

So the baronet set about converting the old and uncouth Arbury Hall into the "Cheverel Manor" of to-day. He laboriously drew out his own designs—which for an amateur architect were considered to be extremely clever, in spite of the mixture of ecclesiastic and richly ornate styles—and entered into a contract with a well-known builder to carry out the scheme.

At that time, which would be about the year 1770, there was a young man employed on the ground, evidently a sort of right-hand man to Sir Roger; for in the renovation and remodelling of the Hall he was eminently useful and in constant request. This young man's name was Robert Evans, the subsequent father of George Eliot ; and it was well for Sir Roger Newdigate, in more ways than one, that he had so trusty a servant upon whom he could rely in his hour of need.

Before the unsightly chambers were hidden by turrets, the beautiful mullioned windows put in, the outer walls encased with stone, the vast courtyard environed with a cloister—in short, some time before Arbury Hall was metamorphosed into its present attractive shape—the man who had contracted to build the place became a bankrupt and brought a sudden cessation to the active work then in progress. Sir Roger for the moment was in a state of great perturbation, but the remarkable tact and ability of Robert Evans stood him in good stead, and the Cheverel Manor as it appears to-day was finished under the watchful eyes of the owner and his steward.

Arbury Hall was probably finished in, or about, 1773, as in that year Sir John Astley, of the adjoining Astley Castle, made Sir Roger Newdigate a present of the famous painting depicting the celebrated exploits of Sir John de Astley, who flourished in the early part of the fifteenth century.

The outside of the mansion, with its castellated grey-tinted front and mullioned windows, is easily recognised by all readers of "Mr. Gilfil's Love Story"; it is in the inside, however, that the descriptions of George Eliot force themselves upon the mind, as the visitor looks with a curious eye upon the ecclesiastical and other adornments placed in their respective positions by the lavish hand of Sir Roger.

The saloon adornments are copied from the fan tracery in Henry the Seventh's Chapel at Westminster. In a similar manner the ceiling of the drawing-room is elaborately carved with tracery in which are inserted different armorial bearings on small shields. The room next to the saloon contains the picture before alluded to. It commemorates the exploits of Sir John de Astley, a famous knight, who vanquished, in a duel at Paris, one Peter de Maise, and in the thirtieth year of Henry the Sixth's reign fought with, and defeated, at Smithfield, an aspiring knight of Aragon, one Sir Philip Boyle, who seems to have been a kind of Don Quixote, anxious to cross swords with some great fighter. A replica of this painting is preserved at Patshull, the seat of the Earl of Dartmouth, a descendant of the Astleys of Warwickshire.

Here and there in the adjacent rooms are many evidences of the classical tastes of Sir Roger Newdigate. There are niches filled with casts from the antique, all breathing of the days when the Gothic-loving baronet was drinking in the inspirations of architectural Florence. You can see the Venus de Medici under an elaborate Gothic canopy; and the top of a sarcophagus, brought from Rome by Sir Roger, upon which is finely sculptured the marriage of Bacchus and Ariadne.

George Eliot has herself well described the dining-room. In her day it was so bare of furniture that it impressed one with its architectural beauty like a cathedral.

"The slight matting and a sideboard in a recess did not detain the eye for a moment from the lofty grained ceiling, with its richly carved pendants, all of creamy white, relieved here and there by touches of gold. On one side this lofty ceiling was supported by pillars and arches, beyond which a lower ceiling, a miniature copy of the higher one, covered the square projection, which, with its three pointed windows, formed the central feature of this building. The room looked less like a place to dine in than a piece of space enclosed simply for the sake of beautiful outline ; and the small dining-table seemed a small and insignificant accident rather than anything connected with the original purpose of the apartment."

During the long lifetime of the late Charles N. Newdigate this room had an air of Conservatism about it as rigid as that possessed by its owner. It was, with the smallest variations, the same room as that so carefully described in " Mr. Gilfil's Love Story."

Sir Roger Newdigate, the man of cultivated mind and exquisite taste, died in 1806 at the age of eighty-eight. With his death the title became extinct. In his will, Sir Roger bequeathed Arbury Hall and the estates to Mr. Francis Parker on condition that he adopted the name of Newdigate; and with a reversion to the father of the late Charles N. Newdigate, who had then come into possession again of the estates at Harefield, and who was enjoined to add the old spelling of the name of Newd*e*gate to that of the Charles Newdigate received at the baptismal font. The name of the late owner of Arbury Hall, therefore, was Charles Newd*e*gate Newd*i*gate.

The little village of Griff, in the vicinity of which George Eliot was born, and in which, as already written, lived the other members of her family, was at the Conquest survey involved with Chilvers Coten. In the third year of the reign of Queen Elizabeth, Griff was purchased by John Giffard, whose grandson, in Dugdale's time, passed it on to Sir John Newdigate, father of Sir Roger; it thus became the property of the Newdigates, and the little parish has continued in their family to the present time.

Mining has been the chief industry carried on at Griff. For more than two centuries coal-mines have been known and worked in the neighbourhood, Bedworth being spoken of by Dugdale as "a place very well known with regard to the coal-mines there."

When the father of the late Charles N. Newdigate settled at Arbury he went energetically into the mining work, and appointed John Evans, uncle to George Eliot, as his mining agent. That was a golden time for Warwickshire coal-owners. Railways had not then stretched their feelers into "The Heart of England," as Michael Drayton happily calls Warwickshire; indeed, the only railway near Griff, or in the shire, was one known as "The Stratford and Moreton Railway," which extended from Stratford-on-Avon in Warwickshire to Moreton-in-the-Marsh in Gloucestershire. Even this one was not for passengers; so that our good ancestors, as can be seen in "Silas Marner," only a little more than half a century ago were obliged to travel chiefly by stage-coach and pack-horse.

The Stratford and Moreton Railway Company was incorporated in 1821. The length of the main line was about sixteen miles, and the branch lines two-and-a-half miles. The capital embarked in this enterprise was £50,000. The principal use made of this railway was the supplying with coal—

brought from the Griff and Bedworth pits—of Moreton, Stow-on-the-Wold, and other parts of the country through which it passed, and for conveying back to Stratford-on-Avon stone and agricultural produce.

This was the only enterprise in the shape of a railway then in use in Warwickshire. It is still to be seen, but it is now disused and overgrown with grass and weeds, a striking instance of a work that soon served its purpose and became obsolete.

Though taking a great interest in the working of railways as the means of carrying the coal from his Griff collieries into the world in and beyond the shire, Mr. Newdigate, father of the late Member for North Warwickshire, was also keenly alive to the importance of canals, which at that time were being introduced. The miles upon miles of navigable watercourses that flow so placidly through this beautiful and classic shire tell of the foresight, knowledge, and skilful engineering abilities of our forefathers.

Something may be said at this point of a canal that passes near George Eliot's neighbourhood, which was constructed in 1830, and in which old Mr. Newdigate took a large share of interest.

During the Parliamentary session of 1829, the Oxford Canal Company obtained powers to improve that part of their canal which lies between Braunston in Warwickshire and Longford in Northamptonshire, and which communicated with the Grand Junction and Coventry canals. The construction of works in this canal was upon the most approved methods in the practice of civil engineering. The bridges and tunnels were made sufficiently capacious to admit of a towing-path on either side and two boats to pass. The canal cut through the high lands at Brinklow, the nearest point to Bedworth and Griff, and Newbold, by means of tunnels, twenty-four feet inside diameter, and over the turnpike road from Rugby to historic Lutterworth, upon an aqueduct of cast-iron. A considerable portion of these works was completed and navigable in 1831.

The elder Mr. Newdigate was so strongly impressed with the idea that canals were to be the future travelling courses of the world, that he had a communication with the Grand Junction cut right up to his Hall at Arbury, and it is said that upon more than one occasion he travelled to and from London by boat. This was a piece of good-humoured enterprise about which Charles N. Newdigate chose to be silent as much as possible, and when he did speak of it he liked to convey the impression that in cutting it his father had the draining of his coal-mines in view; but among those old Griff miners the story is still current, or was until recently, of how "Old Charley's feyther went to Lunnon up the Cut."

Perhaps Mr. Newdigate may only have been a few decades in advance of his time, though the incident at that period was certainly one worthy to have been noted down by the pen of George Eliot; but having already described the foibles of one member of the family, the gifted novelist probably deemed it prudent to stay her hand.

To the commercial interests of Warwickshire, however, canals are of the greatest value; and one cannot think of the many advantages which have been gained to mankind by the use of well-planned watercourses that glide through our fields and streets without thanking their constructors, and wondering why canals are not more generally used.

If the Griff miner, the Bedworth ribbon-weaver, or the Astley worker in bead or jet embroidery were at all bookish, and would read George Eliot's "Scenes of Clerical Life," they would be disposed to say, when next visiting Chilvers Coten Church, "Eh! inna it like": for during the past few years the church has been "restored" back to something like the old condition of "Shepperton Church."

The little village of Chilvers Coten, in the parish of which George Eliot was born, is about one mile from Griff. In the Conquest survey it was rated at eight hides, the woods were one mile and a half in length and one mile in breadth; the whole parish being valued at fifty shillings. At the Dissolution of Monasteries, Chilvers Coten came to the Crown, and was sold to John Fisher and Thomas Dalbridgecourt in the fourth year of Queen Elizabeth's reign. These gentlemen, in 1630, obtained a grant of Court Leet to be held there, so that in those days it must have been a somewhat important parish. In course of time Chilvers Coten, along with the village of Griff, came into the hands of the Newdigates.

The Rev. Henry Hake, who died at Leamington some years ago, at a very advanced age, became Vicar of Chilvers Coten and perpetual curate of Astley in 1844, when George Eliot was in her twenty-fifth year, and he may, in some particulars, have suggested Mr. Gilfil. At that time the population of Chilvers Coten was 2612, the patron of the living being the Lord Chancellor. Mr. Hake buried his first wife in the little graveyard there, and resigned the living in the spring of 1859. The generally recognised prototype of Mr. Gilfil, however, was the Rev. Bernard Ebdell, for forty-two years Vicar of Chilvers Coten, who married Sally Shilton ("Tina."), a collier's daughter, who was brought up and educated by Lady Newdigate at Arbury Hall.

That Bedworth colliery master who called George Eliot a " monstrously clever woman " one day met Mr. John Evans, first cousin to

Mary Ann, the novelist, who spoke to him to the following effect :

John Evans, who was then foreman at the Griff Collieries—the date being some time in 1858—when returning from the pits one evening, met Mrs. Newdigate, the mother of "Old Charley," as the miners always called him, driving along in her carriage. She called to the coachman to stop and beckoned Evans to her side.

"Evans," she said, "I have got a book here—it is called 'Adam Bede '—and I want you to take it home and read it to your father."

He replied that his father "dinna tek much account o' books 'cept the Bible," but if it was the lady's wish that he should read it to his father he would do so.

Evans did take the book home and began to read it, and so clearly had George Eliot drawn her characters, that the old man, even as his son read, perfectly identified the people in his own neighbourhood, and every now and then called them out by name. It was this book which the people of Griff, Bedworth, and Chilvers Coten made so much of at the time; and there is not the shadow of a doubt that all the characters in "Adam Bede" lived, moved, and had their being in this little circle.

At Corley, a pretty little village upon an elevation close to Packington Magna, the ancient seat of the Aylesford family, is to be found the "Hall Farm" in which Martin Poyser took so much pride and at which Adam Bede was always a welcome guest. Indeed, every village within a six-mile ring of Griff is instinct with the life to be found in the works of George Eliot. Which village is "Raveloe" it would be difficult to say, as any one of the pretty cluster to be met with there might pass for it; and although linen-weaving in cottages is almost at an end, the ribbon-weaver is still busy with his tireless loom.

But the stranger amid those rural scenes, should he by any chance be at fault concerning his next move, must not make the mistake of inquiring for "Cheverel Manor" or "Shepperton," or he will be met with the truly George Eliot reply of "You mun be cum wrong; I hanna heered of them places."

"If stationary men (and women) would pay

some attention to the districts on which they reside, and would publish their thoughts respecting the objects that surround them, from such materials might be drawn the most complete county histories."

Thus wrote Gilbert White in the first edition of "The Natural History of Selborne," and this evidently was the opinion of George Eliot. In the pleasing form of fiction she has, in her "Scenes of Clerical Life," and other works, furnished material of the highest utility to the writer of county history. She has done even more than that. She has painted pictures of country manners in Warwickshire at the commencement of the nineteenth century which will prove of great value to the Dugdale of the future, and for which she will rank high among those few English novelists who have not made fiction merely a vehicle of amusement.

And there is yet room in Warwickshire for more Walter Scotts, Nathaniel Hawthornes, Washington Irvings, and George Eliots. A county in which almost each noble mansion or venerable ruin, from the princely Warwick Castle to the rugged relics of Kenilworth, carries with it a romance and a history, ought to possess the greatest attraction for the wielder of the pen of romance who can produce a " Kenilworth," or the more quiet, though not less important, writer, who finds a message in the creation of " Scenes of Clerical Life," and the more powerful " Adam Bede."

THE END